An Inspiring Collection of Writings
About the Glory And Greatness of America

NELSON'S PATRIOTIC SCRAPBOOK

"A Past to Remember—a Future to Mold."

Clinton T. Howell
Compiler and Editor

THOMAS NELSON INC., PUBLISHERS
Nashville, Tenn. • New York, New York

Acknowledgment

The generous responses to requests to reprint the material in this volume were gladdening indeed. Our appreciation is hereby expressed to all.

To those authors, representatives, and publishers who have allowed us to use their work without charge, to those who allowed us special arrangement, and to those whose work is now in the public domain, we are deeply grateful.

Some, after diligent search, we were unable to contact. Should there be such—whose work appears here without proper arrangement or acknowledgment—please allow us to make such in the next printing. It is not our desire or intention to use anyone's material without permission or proper credit.

Acknowledgment is made to the following who have, through special arrangement, granted permission to use copyrighted material:

AMERICAN LEGION MAGAZINE for "Benjamin Franklin, Diplomat of the Revolution" by Harvey Ardman.

DENVER POST for "Sacred Hall of Independence" by Paul Friggens.

FOLLETT PUBLISHING COMPANY for "Thomas Jefferson: A Day to Remember" by Clara Ingram Judson.

McCALL COMPANY for "Lincoln Goes to Gettysburg" by Carl Sandburg.

RICHMOND TIMES-DISPATCH for "A Giant of the Revolution" by Nancy Hale.

UNITED NEWSPAPER MAGAZINE CORPORATION for "All Over, Over There"; "Gotterdammerung in Germany"; "The Rising Sun Goes Down"; "Washington's Greatest Triumph" and "The Worst Day of My Life" all by Thomas Fleming. Painting of "V-J Day 1945" by Isa Barnett.

Printed in the United States of America

Library of Congress Cataloging in Publication Data

Howell, Clinton Talmage, 1913- comp.
Nelson's patriotic scrapbook.

1. United States—History—Miscellanea. I. Title.
II. Title: Patriotic scrapbook,
E179.H85 973 74-5439
ISBN 8407-5567-8

Preface

July 4 is America's Birthday, for on that day in 1776, fifty-six stalwart men signed the *Declaration of Independence,* pledging their lives, their fortunes, and their sacred honor to such things as liberty, equality, brotherhood, and the common good. As subjects of England, these signers were committing an act of treason—the penalty, death by hanging.

The young nation faltered at first but never failed. The ideals, convictions, devotion and courage of strong-hearted men sustained the glorious undertaking, which has lived and increased to fulfill the grand American dream of freedom, freedom of religion and press, freedom from want, fear and tyranny—freedoms which have hallowed our own Nation and have extended their beneficent influence to all Nations—all mankind.

The generation from the 1760's to the close of the century accomplished two very great things: it won independence, and it established a nation. Of these the first—the winning of independence—has always commanded the livelier interest and the deeper admiration. But the greatest single achievement of Americans of this generation was that they laid the foundations for a nation that provided order, justice, and freedom for millions of people, that spread over a whole continent, and that has endured to our own time.

We take all this for granted, but should we? After all, South America won independence from Spain but divided into twenty-three nations. When George Washington took the oath of office as the first President of the United States, Louis XVI reigned in France; there was a Holy Roman Emperor, a Russian Czar, an absolute monarch in Sweden and in Denmark, a Sultan in Turkey, and an Emperor in China. All these have been swept away down the swift current of history. Yet the American nation is today the oldest republic, the oldest federal system, the oldest democracy in the world, and its Constitution is the oldest written constitution in the world.

During this forty-year period, the pen was truly mightier than the sword—or, for that matter, than the plow or the sail or the coin. Independence was won as much by the fiery rhetoric of Thomas Paine's *Common Sense* and the exalted eloquence of the *Declaration of Independence* as by the weapons of Washington or Lafayette. Without *Common Sense* and *The Crisis* there might have been no army for Washington to lead; without the *Declaration of Independence* and the other writings of Jefferson, France might never have joined the war. Other nations—England, France, Germany—were hammered together on the anvil of war, but the thirteen original American states were persuaded to become a single nation by the peaceful arguments of statesmen and men of letters.

Appropriately, NELSON'S PATRIOTIC SCRAPBOOK is an "anthology of American Democracy," in loose chronological succession, of the thrilling historical record and fact of men, movements and moments, of the march of America, from Concord to Philadelphia, from Yorktown to Appomatox, from the Clermont to the Apollo, and to the Moon and beyond. Words of statesmen and men of letters, the great documents, anthems and illustrations are here recording the heritage, the achievements, the hopes and horizon of our goodly land.

We are challenged therefore to move confidently onward, into a creative tomorrow for a unified Nation and a unified world, of understanding, goodwill and peace, with liberty and justice for all mankind. "We love our land for what she is, and what she is to be."

Should this volume aid in urging your love, loyalty and devotion to your country—the United States of America—we shall be remarkably rewarded.

Clinton T. Howell

Nashville, Tennessee

Contents

The Colonial Time

THE LANDING OF THE PILGRIMS

They laid the foundation
of a state wherein every man
through countless ages
should have liberty.

INSCRIPTION ON
PLYMOUTH ROCK MONUMENT

THE PILGRIM FATHERS

A few years after James became king, a number of the Separatists living in the village of Scrooby, England, made up their minds to form a church of their own. They used to meet for worship every week in the home of William Brewster, one of their members. When the king heard of this he was displeased. "Since these men do not obey me," he declared, "they must be punished." Some of them were thrown into prison and some were hanged.

But the Separatists believed they were right, and bravely decided to leave their country and go to Holland, where they knew they would be allowed to worship God as they pleased. First they went to Amsterdam, then to Leyden, and at last to America by way of England. On account of their wanderings they were called Pilgrims.

In Holland they worked so hard and were so honest that they won the respect and good will of the Dutch. Nevertheless they were not happy, for they could not bear to see their children growing up in Dutch ways and speaking the Dutch language. They longed to go to a new country where they could train their boys and girls to be English in language, manners, and habits. They decided, therefore, to seek homes in the New World.

But, as is often true with us of to-day, it was easier to plan than to carry out. In the first place, King James was not willing that they should again live in a country under his rule, though at length he agreed not to disturb them in America if they gave him no trouble. In the second place, ready as they were to brave any danger, they were too poor to pay for their enterprise. But this difficulty too was overcome. They borrowed money, although on hard terms, and set sail from Delfthaven in the *Speedwell* for Plymouth, England. Here they found some friends who were to join them, and a small ship, the *Mayflower*, which had been hired in London.

After some delay, they put to sea in the two small ships, but on account of a leak the *Speedwell* had to return. Finally, on September 6, 1620, with one hundred and two passengers, they set sail. Then followed a long and stormy voyage. Not until Saturday, November 21, after being at sea sixty-four days, did the Pilgrims anchor safely in the harbor of what is now the village of Provincetown, Mass.

We on this continent should never forget that men first crossed the Atlantic not to find soil for their ploughs but to secure liberty for their souls.

ROBERT J. MCCRACKEN

THE "MAYFLOWER"

SYMBOLIC APPROACH

Each of us has made his symbolic approach to Plymouth Rock; each is here because someone took a step forward and felt a sustaining firmness underfoot, whether the landing took place from the *Mayflower*, from an Irish "coffin ship," on Ellis Island, or from the last jet at Logan or LaGuardia.

FRANCIS RUSSELL

THE MAYFLOWER COMPACT

Signed in the Cabin of the *Mayflower*, Nov. 11th, Old Style, Nov. 21st, New Style, 1620

"In the name of God, amen, we whose names are underwritten, the loyall subjects of our dread soveraigne Lord, King James, by the grace of God, of Great Britaine, Franc and Ireland king, defender of the faith, &c., haveing undertaken, for the glorie of God, and advancemente of the Christian faith, and honor of our king and countrie, a voyage to plant the first colonie in the northerne parts of Virginia, doe by these presents solemnly and mutualy in the presence of God, and of one another, covenant and combine ourselves together into a civill body politick, for our better ordering and preservation and furtherence of the ends aforesaid; and by vertue hereof to enacte, constitute and frame such just and equall laws, ordenances, acts, constitutions and offices, from time to time, as shall be thought most meete and convenient for the general good of the colonie, unto which we promise all due submission and obedience. In witness whereof we have hereunto subscribed our names at Cap-Codd the 11 of November, in the year of the raigne of our soveraigne lord, King James of England, Franc and Ireland the eighteenth, and of Scotland the fifty-fourth, ANo Dom 1620."

When England grew corrupt, God brought over a number of pious persons and planted them in New England, and this land was planted with a noble vine.

JONATHAN EDWARDS

HEROES OF FAITH

By faith the voyaging *Mayflower* embarked from Old England and found harbor off the bleak New England shores. By faith the Pilgrim Fathers set up a government on a new continent dedicated to God and inspired by a desire to do his will on earth as it is done in heaven.

By faith Thomas Jefferson was stirred to strike a blow for political independence and wrote the thrilling document that declared that all men are created equal and endowed with certain inalienable rights. By faith he said, "Love your neighbor as yourself and your country more than yourself."

By faith George Washington left his spacious mansion at Mount Vernon and espoused the cause of the tax-burdened colonists. By faith he forsook ease and comfort, choosing rather to suffer hardship with his men at Valley Forge than to enjoy the favor of a king. By faith he became the President of the newly born republic and endured as seeing Him who is invisible.

By faith Alexander Hamilton established the financial credit of the nation. In the eloquent words of Daniel Webster: "He touched the corpse of public credit and it sprang into life. He smote the rock of national resources and abundant streams of revenue flowed." By faith James Madison gave richly of his scholarly mind to form the Federal Constitution. By faith Andrew Jackson fought the battle of the impoverished and underprivileged many against the privileged few.

By faith Abraham Lincoln bore the awful burden of four purgatorial years seeking to preserve the Federal Union. By faith he carried a dreadful war to its conclusion without hate in his heart, saying, "I have not only suffered for the South, I have suffered with the South."

By faith Woodrow Wilson in the dreadful heartbreak of a world war dreamed a dream of a warless world in which the nations should be leagued together to keep the peace. By faith he glimpsed that promised land which, like Moses, he might not enter.

And what shall I more say? For time would fail me if I should tell of that unnumbered host, the unnamed and obscure citizens who bore unimagined burdens, sacrificed in silence and endured nobly, that a government of the people, for the people, and by the people might not perish from the earth.

EDGAR DE WITT JONES

. . . The heavy night hung dark
The hills and waters o'er,
When a band of exiles moored their bark
On the wild New England shore.

Not as the conqueror comes,
They, the true-hearted came:
Not with the roll of the stirring drums,
And the trumpet that sings of fame. . . .

What sought they thus afar?
Bright jewels of the mine?
The wealth of seas, the spoils of war? —
They sought a faith's pure shrine.

From "Landing of the Pilgrim Fathers" by Felicia Hemans.

THE PILGRIMS GOING TO CHURCH

THE LANDING OF COLUMBUS

Columbus

Behind him lay the gray Azores,
Behind the Gates of Hercules;
Before him not the ghost of shores,
Before him only shoreless seas.
The good mate said: "Now must we pray,
For lo! the very stars are gone.
Brave Adm'r'l, speak; what shall I say?"
"Why, say: "Sail on! sail on! and on!' "

"My men grow mutinous day by day;
My men grow ghastly wan and weak."
The stout mate thought of home; a spray
Of salt wave washed his swarthy cheek.
"What shall I say, brave Adm'r'l, say,
If we sight naught but seas at dawn?"
"Why, you shall say, at break of day:
'Sail on! sail on! sail on! and on!' "

They sailed and sailed, as winds might blow,
Until at last the blanched mate said:
"Why, now not even God would know
Should I and all my men fall dead.
These very winds forget their way,
For God from these dread seas is gone.
Now speak, brave Adm'r'l; speak and say"—
He said: "Sail on! sail on! and on!"

They sailed. They sailed. Then spake the mate:
"This mad sea shows his teeth to-night;
He curled his lips, he lies in wait,
With lifted teeth, as if to bite:
Brave Adm'r'l, say but one good word;
What shall we do when hope is gone?"
The words leapt like a leaping sword:
"Sail on! sail on! sail on! and on!"

Then, pale and worn, he kept his deck,
And peered through darkness. Ah, that night
Of all dark nights! And then a speck—
A light! a light! a light! a light!
It grew, a starlit flag unfurled!
It grew to be Time's burst of dawn.
He gained a world; he gave that world
Its grandest lesson: "On! sail on!"

CINCINNATUS HINER MILLER
Known as JOAQUIN MILLER

What the early Puritans gave American culture amounts to much more than the " blue laws," the witch-hunting, and the stern religious doctrine for which they are now all too commonly known.

The Puritans gave us free public education, a thoroughgoing respect for learning, our first books and our first college, and the habit of representative government.

That they had time for intellectual concerns is remarkable. They were faced not only with the formidable tasks of conquering the wilderness and setting up trade, but with providing for such physical necessities as food, clothing, and shelter. Yet they did not lose sight of the value of the printed page. As early as 1640 a printing press was turning out books. Taxes were levied for public education. There could not be a learned clergy without a college. Accordingly, in 1636 Harvard College was founded, named for John Harvard, who gave his library to it.

It was Puritan Roger Williams who established the tradition of religious freedom in America. He was banned from the Massachusetts Bay Colony because he argued that one need not support a church in which he was not in complete agreement. He had also written a pamphlet saying that the King of England had no right to grant Indian lands to colonists. He fled from Salem and was welcomed by friendly Indians from whom he bought land. With a few followers he founded the town of Providence in 1636.

We have a right to be proud of our Pilgrim and Puritan fathers. They were ready to do and to suffer anything for their faith, and a faith which breeds heroes is better than an unbelief which leaves nothing worth being a hero for.

OLIVER WENDELL HOLMES

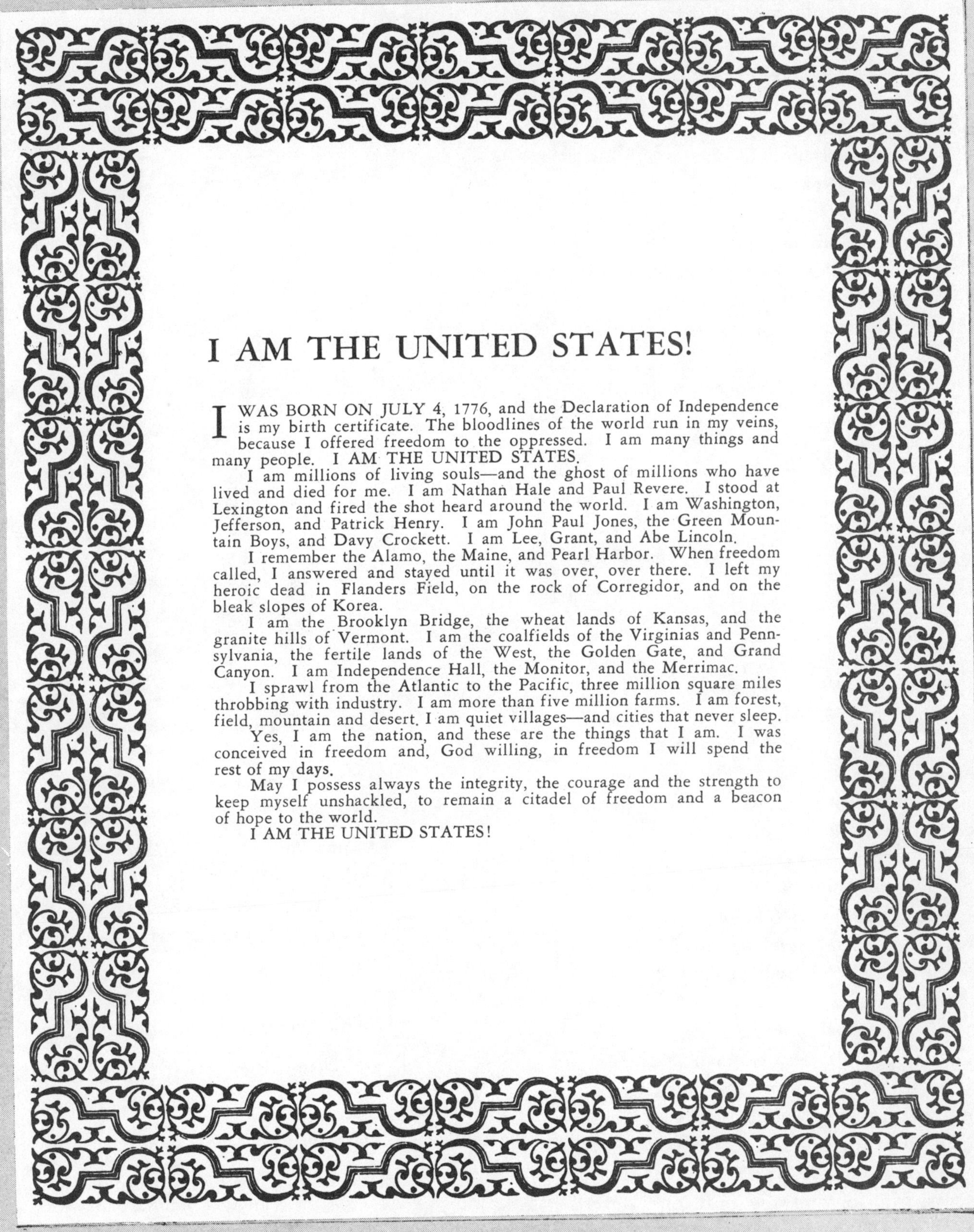

I AM THE UNITED STATES!

I WAS BORN ON JULY 4, 1776, and the Declaration of Independence is my birth certificate. The bloodlines of the world run in my veins, because I offered freedom to the oppressed. I am many things and many people. I AM THE UNITED STATES.

I am millions of living souls—and the ghost of millions who have lived and died for me. I am Nathan Hale and Paul Revere. I stood at Lexington and fired the shot heard around the world. I am Washington, Jefferson, and Patrick Henry. I am John Paul Jones, the Green Mountain Boys, and Davy Crockett. I am Lee, Grant, and Abe Lincoln.

I remember the Alamo, the Maine, and Pearl Harbor. When freedom called, I answered and stayed until it was over, over there. I left my heroic dead in Flanders Field, on the rock of Corregidor, and on the bleak slopes of Korea.

I am the Brooklyn Bridge, the wheat lands of Kansas, and the granite hills of Vermont. I am the coalfields of the Virginias and Pennsylvania, the fertile lands of the West, the Golden Gate, and Grand Canyon. I am Independence Hall, the Monitor, and the Merrimac.

I sprawl from the Atlantic to the Pacific, three million square miles throbbing with industry. I am more than five million farms. I am forest, field, mountain and desert. I am quiet villages—and cities that never sleep.

Yes, I am the nation, and these are the things that I am. I was conceived in freedom and, God willing, in freedom I will spend the rest of my days.

May I possess always the integrity, the courage and the strength to keep myself unshackled, to remain a citadel of freedom and a beacon of hope to the world.

I AM THE UNITED STATES!

WILLIAM PENN'S LEGACY

William Penn spent less than four years in the colonies. Yet his influence on their development and his legacy to the future United States were as important a contribution as that made by any settler or other English promoter of the 17th Century.

He shared prominently in establishing three colonies—New Jersey, Delaware, and Pennsylvania.

He saw that humble folk got a chance to start their lives anew under favorable conditions.

He practiced and preached religious freedom.

He was a great humanitarian in an inhumane age.

He wrought so well that his ideals have in the long course of time become primary ingredients in the tradition of democracy in America.

CARL BRIDENBAUGH

TREATY WITH THE INDIANS

"We meet," said William Penn, "on the broad pathway of good faith and good will; no advantage shall be taken on either side, but all shall be openness and love. The friendship between you and me I will not compare to a chain; for that the rains might rust or the falling tree might break. We are the same as if one man's body were to be divided into two parts; we are all one flesh and blood."

"We will live in love with William Penn and his children," said the Indians, "as long as the sun and moon shall shine."

The simple-minded natives kept the history of this treaty by means of strings of wampum, and they would often count over the shells on a clean piece of bark and rehearse its provisions. "It was the only treaty never sworn to, and the only one never broken." On every hand the Indians waged relentless war with the colonies, but they never shed a drop of Quaker blood.

A BRIEF HISTORY OF THE UNITED STATES (1871)

Roger Williams, founder of Providence and father of religious freedom.

To proclaim a true and absolute soul freedom to all the people of the land impartially so that no person be forced to pray, nor pray otherwise than as his soul believeth and consenteth.

ROGER WILLIAMS

The Pocahontas Incident

Captain John Smith's most famous adventure was his narrow escape from death at the hands of the Indians when the princess Pocahontas intervened to save his life. Historians suspect that the doughty captain embellished this romantic episode with his imagination. True or not, the story is generally accepted by Americans. Smith writes in the third person; Captain Smith is the " him " we find a prisoner of the savages.

AT LAST he was brought to Meronocomoco, where was Powhatan their Emperor. Here more than two hundred of those grim courtiers stood wondering at him, as he had been a monster; [1] till Powhatan and his train had put themselves in their greatest braveries.[2] Before a fire upon a seat like a bedstead, he [3] sat covered with a great robe, made of raccoon skins, and all the tails hanging by. On either hand did sit a young wench of sixteen or eighteen years, and along on each side the house, two rows of men, and behind them as many women, with all their heads and shoulders painted red; many of their heads bedecked with the white down of birds; but every one with something: and a great chain of white beads about their necks.

At his entrance before the King, all the people gave a great shout. The Queen of Appamatuck was appointed to bring him water to wash his hands, and another brought him a bunch of feathers, instead of a towel, to dry them. Having feasted him after their best barbarous manner they could, a long consultation was held, but the conclusion was, two great stones were brought before Powhatan: then as many as could laid hands on him, dragged him to them, and thereon laid his head, and being ready with their clubs to beat out his brains, Pocahontas the King's dearest daughter, when no entreaty could prevail, got his head in her arms, and laid her own upon his to save him from death: whereat the Emperor was contented he should live to make him hatchets, and [to make] her bells, beads, and copper; for they thought him as well of all occupations [4] as themselves. For the King himself will make his own robes, shoes, bows, arrows, pots; plant, hunt, or do anything so well as the rest.

Two days after, Powhatan having disguised himself in the most fearfulest manner he could, caused Captain Smith to be brought forth to a great house in the woods, and there upon a mat by the fire to be left alone. Not long after from behind a mat that divided the house, was made the most dolefulest noise he ever heard: then Powhatan more like a devil than a man, with some two hundred more as black as himself, came unto him and told him now they were friends, and presently he should go to Jamestown, to send him two great guns and a grindstone, for which he would give him the County of Capahowosick, and forever esteem him as his son Nantaquoud.

Sacred to the Memory of
John Cooke
Who was buried here in 1695
The last surviving male Pilgrim
Of those who came over in the
Mayflower
The first white settler of this town
And the pioneer in its religious
Moral and business life
A man of character and integrity
And the trusted agent for this
Part of the Commonwealth
Of the Old Colonial
Civil Government of Plymouth.

COOKE MEMORIAL PARK
FAIRHAVEN, MASSACHUSETTS

EPITAPH TO LUCY EATON

Descended from the Pilgrims
She lov'd their doctrines
And practic'd their virtues.

MIDDLE CEMETERY
LANCASTER, MASSACHUSETTS

A nation is made great, not by its fruitful acres, but by the men who cultivate them; not by its great forests, but by the men who use them; not by its mines, but by the men who build and run them. America was a great land when Columbus discovered it; Americans have made of it a great nation.

LYMAN ABBOTT

PRAYER

God of our fathers, give unto us, thy servants, a true appreciation of our heritage, of great men and great deeds in the past, but let us not be intimidated by feelings of our own inadequacy for this troubled hour.

Remind us that the God they worshiped, and by whose help they laid the foundations of our Nation, is still able to help us uphold what they bequeathed and to give it new meanings.

Remind us that we are not called to fill the places of those who have gone, but to fill our own places, to do the work thou hast laid before us, to do the right as thou hast given us to see the right, always to do the very best we can, and to leave the rest to thee.

PETER MARSHALL

THE PILGRIM FATHERS

O God, beneath thy guiding hand
Our exiled fathers crossed the sea;
And when they trod the wintry strand,
With prayer and psalm they worshipped thee.

Thou heard'st, well pleased, the song, the prayer:
Thy blessing came; and still its power
Shall onward through all ages bear
The memory of that holy hour.

Laws, freedom, truth, and faith in God
Came with those exiles o'er the waves;
And where their pilgrim feet have trod,
The God they trusted guards their graves.

And here thy name, O, God of love,
Their children's children shall adore,
Till these eternal hills remove,
And spring adorns the earth no more.

LEONARD BACON

Paul Revere made this engraving of Harvard College, drawn by Joseph Chadwick.

Essex Institute

The Making of a Nation

By the rude bridge that arched the flood,
Their flag to April's breeze unfurled,
Here once the embattled farmers stood,
And fired the shot heard round the world.

RALPH WALDO EMERSON

The Boston Massacre March 5, 1770

The Concord Hymn

Today at Concord you can see a graceful bridge, and near it, through the trees, the famous bronze statue of the Minute Man. At its base is carved the first stanza of "The Concord Hymn."

On July 4, 1837, Ralph Waldo Emerson stood at this bridge and read his poem on the dedication of the original monument, at the other end of the bridge, commemorating the Battle of Concord, which opened the American Revolution.

Emerson and his Concord neighbors were determined that the battle of 1775 should be remembered "when, like our sires, our sons are gone." Emerson's poem turned the trick; the "shot heard round the world" is indeed immortal.

By the rude bridge that arched the flood,
Their flag to April's breeze unfurled,
Here once the embattled farmers stood,
And fired the shot heard round the world.

The foe long since in silence slept;
Alike the conqueror silent sleeps;
And Time the ruined bridge has swept
Down the dark stream which seaward creeps.

On this green bank, by this soft stream,
We set today a votive stone;
That memory may their deed redeem,
When, like our sires, our sons are gone.

Spirit, that made those heroes dare
To die and leave their children free,
Bid Time and Nature gently spare
The shaft we raise to them and thee.

SOWING THE DRAGON'S TEETH

They started for The Ship and Anchor with a number of men and boys following and trying to talk with them.

"I'll tell ye, Jack, they's trouble ahead," said Solomon as they made their way through the crowded streets.

Many were saying that there could be no more peace with England.

In the morning they learned that three men had been killed and five others wounded by the soldiers. Squads of men and boys with loaded muskets were marching into town from the country.

Jack and Solomon attended the town meeting that day in the old South Meeting-House. It was a quiet and orderly crowd that listened to the speeches of Josiah Quincy, John Hancock and Samuel Adams, demanding calmly but firmly that the soldiers be forthwith removed from the city. The famous John Hancock cut a great figure in Boston those days. It is not surprising that Jack was impressed by his grandeur for he had entered the meeting-house in a scarlet velvet cap and a blue damask gown lined with velvet and strode to the platform with a dignity even above his garments. As he faced about the boy did not fail to notice and admire the white satin waistcoat and white silk stockings and red morocco slippers. Mr. Quincy made a statement which stuck like a bur in Jack Irons' memory of that day and perhaps all the faster because he did not quite understand it. The speaker said: "The dragon's teeth have been sown."

The chairman asked if there was any citizen present who had been on the scene at or about the time of the shooting. Solomon Binkus arose and held up his hand and was asked to go to the minister's room and confer with the committee.

Mr. John Adams called at the inn that evening and announced that he was to defend Captain Preston and would require the help of Jack and Solomon as witnesses. For that reason they were detained some days in Boston and released finally on the promise to return when their services were required.

Irving Bacheller

The Boston Massacre
March 5, 1770

The Boston Gazette and Country Journal, March 12, 1770.

The town of Boston affords a recent and melancholy demonstration of the destructive consequences of quartering troops among citizens in a time of peace, under a pretence of supporting the laws and aiding civil authority; every considerate and unprejudiced person among us was deeply impressed with the apprehension of these consequences when it was known that a number of regiments were ordered to this town under such a pretext, but in reality to enforce oppressive measures; to awe and control the legislative as well as executive power of the province, and to quell a spirit of liberty, which however it may have been basely opposed and even ridiculed by some, would do honour to any age or country. A few persons amongst us had determined to use all their influence to procure so destructive a measure with a view to their securely enjoying the profits of an American revenue, and unhappily both for Britain and this country they found means to effect it.

It is to Governor Bernard, the commissioners, their confidants and coadjutors, that we are indebted as the procuring cause of a military power in this capital. The Boston Journal of Occurrences, as printed in Mr. Holt's *New York Gazette*, from time to time, afforded many striking instances of the distresses brought upon the inhabitants by this measure; and since those Journals have been discontinued, our troubles from that quarter have been growing upon us. We have known a party of soldiers in the face of day fire off a loaden musket upon the inhabitants, others have been pricked with bayonets, and even our magistrates assaulted and put in danger of their lives, when offenders brought before them have been rescued; and why those and other bold and base criminals have as yet escaped the punishment due to their crimes may be soon matter of enquiry by the representative body of this people. It is natural to suppose that when the inhabitants of this town saw those laws which had been enacted for their security, and which they were ambitious of holding up to the soldiery, eluded, they should more commonly resent for themselves; and accordingly it has so happened. Many have been the squabbles between them and the soldiery; but it seems their being often worsted by our youth in those rencounters, has only served to irritate the former. What passed at Mr. Gray's rope-walk has already been given the public and may be said to have led the way to the late catastrophe. That the rope-walk lads, when attacked by superior numbers, should defend themselves with so much spirit and success in the club-way, was too mortifying, and perhaps it may hereafter appear that even some of their

FANEUIL HALL, "THE CRADLE OF LIBERTY."
(This building was dedicated by Otis in 1763.)

From BOSTON

We grant no dukedoms to the few,
  We hold like rights and shall;
Equal on Sunday in the pew,
  On Monday in the mall.
For what avail the plough or sail,
Or land, or life, if freedom fail?

RALPH WALDO EMERSON

CONCORD BRIDGE AS IT IS TO-DAY

officers were unhappily affected with this circumstance. Divers stories were propagated among the soldiery that served to agitate their spirits; particularly on the Sabbath that one Chambers, a sergeant, represented as a sober man, had been missing the preceding day and must therefore have been murdered by the townsmen. An officer of distinction so far credited this report that he entered Mr. Gray's rope-walk that Sabbath; and when required of by that gentleman as soon as he could meet him, the occasion of his so doing, the officer replied that it was to look if the sergeant said to be murdered had not been hid there. This sober sergeant was found on the Monday unhurt in a house of pleasure. The evidences already collected show that many threatenings had been thrown out by the soldiery, but we do not pretend to say that there was any preconcerted plan. When the evidences are published, the world will judge. We may, however, venture to declare that it appears too probable from their conduct that some of the soldiery aimed to draw and provoke the townsmen into squabbles, and that they then intended to make use of other weapons than canes, clubs, or bludgeons.

Our readers will doubtless expect a circumstantial account of the tragical affair on Monday night last; but we hope they will excuse our being so particular as we should have been, had we not seen that the town was intending an enquiry and full representation thereof.

On the evening of Monday, being the fifth current, several soldiers of the 29th Regiment were seen parading the streets with their drawn cutlasses and bayonets, abusing and wounding numbers of the inhabitants.

A few minutes after nine o'clock four youths, named Edward Archbald, William Merchant, Francis Archbald, and John Leech, jun., came down Cornhill together, and separating at Doctor Loring's corner, the two former were passing the narrow alley leading to Murray's barrack in which was a soldier brandishing a broad sword of an uncommon size against the walls, out of which he struck fire plentifully. A person of mean countenance armed with a large cudgel bore him company. Edward Archbald admonished Mr. Merchant to take care of the sword, on which the soldier turned round and struck Archbald on the arm, then pushed at Merchant and pierced through his clothes inside the arm close to the armpit and grazed the skin. Merchant then struck the soldier with a short stick he had; and the other person ran to the barrack and brought with him two soldiers, one armed with a pair of tongs, the other with a shovel. He with the tongs pursued Archbald back through the alley, collared and laid him over the head with the tongs. The noise brought people together; and John Hicks, a young lad, coming up, knocked the soldier down but let him get up again; and more lads gathering, drove them back to the barrack where the boys stood some time as it were to keep them in. In less than a minute ten or twelve of them came out with drawn cutlasses, clubs, and bayonets and set upon the unarmed boys and young folk who stood them a little while but, finding the inequality of their equipment, dispersed. On hearing the noise, one Samuel Atwood came up to see what was the matter; and entering the alley from dock square, heard the latter part of the combat; and when the boys had dispersed he met the ten or twelve soldiers aforesaid rushing down the alley towards the square and asked them if they intended to murder people? They answered Yes, by G-d, root and branch! With that one of them struck Mr. Atwood with a club which was repeated by another; and being unarmed, he turned to go off and received a wound on the left shoulder which reached the bone and gave him much pain. Retreating a few steps, Mr. Atwood met two officers and said, gentlemen, what is the matter? They answered, you'll see by and by. Immediately after, those heroes appeared in the square, asking where were the boogers? where were the cowards? But notwithstanding their fierceness to naked men, one of them advanced towards a youth who had a split of a raw stave in his hand and said, damn them, here is one of them. But the young man seeing a person near him with a drawn sword and good cane ready to support him, held up his stave in defiance; and they quietly passed by him up the little alley by Mr. Silsby's to King Street where they attacked single and unarmed persons till they raised much clamour, and then turned down Cornhill Street, insulting all they met in like manner and pursuing some to their very doors. Thirty or forty persons, mostly lads, being by this means gathered in King Street, Capt. Preston with a party of men with charged bayonets, came from the main guard to the commissioner's house, the soldiers pushing their bayonets, crying, make way! They took place by the custom house and, continuing to push to drive the people off, pricked some in several places, on which they were clamorous and, it is said, threw snow balls. On this, the Captain commanded them to fire; and more snow balls coming, he again said, damn you, fire, be the consequence what it will! One soldier then fired, and a townsman with a cudgel struck him over the hands with such force that he dropped his firelock; and, rushing forward, aimed a blow at the Captain's head which grazed his hat and fell pretty heavy upon his arm. However, the soldiers continued the fire successively till seven or eight or, as some say, eleven guns were discharged.

By this fatal manœuvre three men were laid dead on the spot and two more struggling for life; but what showed a degree of cruelty unknown to British troops, at least since the house of Hanover has directed their operations, was an attempt to fire upon or push with their bayonets the persons who undertook to remove the slain and wounded!

Mr. Benjamin Leigh, now undertaker in the Delph manufactory, came up; and after some conversation with Capt. Preston relative to his conduct in this affair, advised him to draw off his men, with which he complied.

The dead are Mr. Samuel Gray, killed on the spot, the ball entering his head and beating off a large portion of his skull.

A mulatto man named Crispus Attucks, who was born in Framingham, but lately belonged to New-Providence and was here in order to go for North Carolina, also killed instantly, two balls entering his breast, one of them in special goring the right lobe of the lungs and a great part of the liver most horribly.

Mr. James Caldwell, mate of Capt. Morton's vessel, in like manner killed by two balls entering his back.

Mr. Samuel Maverick, a promising youth of seventeen years of age, son of the widow Maverick, and an apprentice to Mr. Greenwood, ivory-turner, mortally wounded; a ball went through his belly and was cut out at his back. He died the next morning.

A lad named Christopher Monk, about seventeen years of age, an apprentice to Mr. Walker, shipwright, wounded; a ball entered his back about four inches above the left kidney near the spine and was cut out of the breast on the same side. Apprehended he will die.

A lad named John Clark, about seventeen years of age, whose parents live at Medford, and an apprentice to Capt. Samuel Howard of this town, wounded; a ball entered just above his groin and came out at his hip on the opposite side. Apprehended he will die.

Mr. Edward Payne of this town, merchant, standing at his entry door received a ball in his arm which shattered some of the bones.

Mr. John Green, tailor, coming up Leverett's Lane, received a ball just under his hip and lodged in the under part of his thigh, which was extracted.

Mr. Robert Patterson, a seafaring man, who was the person that had his trousers shot through in Richardson's affair, wounded; a ball went through his right arm, and he suffered a great loss of blood.

Mr. Patrick Carr, about thirty years of age, who worked with Mr. Field, leather breeches-maker in Queen Street, wounded; a ball entered near his hip and went out at his side.

☆☆☆☆☆

At eleven o'clock the inhabitants met at Faneuil Hall; and after some animated speeches becoming the occasion, they chose a committee of fifteen respectable gentlemen to wait upon the lieutenant-governor in Council to request of him to issue his orders for the immediate removal of the troops.

PAUL REVERE'S RIDE

From PAUL REVERE'S RIDE

So through the night rode Paul Revere;
And so through the night went his cry of
alarm
To every Middlesex village and farm,
A cry of defiance, and not of fear,
A voice in the darkness, a knock at the door,
And a word that shall echo forevermore!
For, borne on the night-wind of the Past,
Through all our history, to the last,
In the hour of darkness and peril and need,
The people will waken and listen to hear
The hurrying hoof-beats of that steed,
And the midnight message of Paul Revere.

HENRY WADSWORTH LONGFELLOW

HE RODE INTO HISTORY

So away, down the moonlit road, goes Paul Revere and the Larkin horse, galloping into history; art, editorials, folklore, poetry; the beat of those hooves never to be forgotten. The man, his bold dark face bent, his hands light on the reins, his body giving to the flowing rhythm beneath him, becoming, as it were, something greater than himself—not merely one man riding one horse on a certain lonely night of long ago, but a symbol to which his countrymen can yet turn. Paul Revere had started on a ride which, in a way, has never ended.

ESTHER FORBES
From PAUL REVERE AND THE WORLD
HE LIVED IN

Battle of Lexington
April 19, 1775

Pennsylvania Journal, May 24, 1775.

About ten o'clock last night, the troops in Boston were discovered to be in motion in a very secret manner, and it was found they were embarking in boats which they had privately brought to the place in the evening at the lower end of the common. Expresses set off immediately to alarm the country, that they might be on their guard. When they were passing about a mile beyond Lexington, they were stopped by a party of officers who came out of Boston in the afternoon of that day, and were seen lurking in bye-places in the country until after dark. One of the expresses immediately fled, and was pursued a long distance by an officer, who, when he had overtaken him, presented a pistol and cried out, "You're a dead man if you don't stop!" but he kept on until he gained a house, when, stopping suddenly, he was thrown from his horse; and having the presence of mind to call out to the people of the house, "Turn out! turn out! I've got one of them!" the officer immediately retreated as fast as he had pursued. The other express [Paul Revere] after undergoing a strict examination, was allowed to depart.

The body of the troops, in the mean time, under the command of Lieutenant-Colonel Smith, had crossed the river and landed at Phipps' farm. They proceeded with great silence to Lexington, six miles below Concord. A company of militia, numbering about eighty men, had mustered near the meetinghouse. Just before sunrise the King's troops came in sight, when the militia began to disperse. The troops then set out upon the road, hallooing and huzzaing, and coming within a few rods of them, the commanding officer cried out in words to this effect, "Disperse, you damned rebels! damn you, disperse!" upon which the troops again huzzaed, and at the same time one or two officers discharged their pistols, which were instantaneously followed by the firing of four or five of the soldiers, and then there seemed to be a general discharge from the whole. It is to be noticed, they fired upon the militia as they were dispersing agreeably to their command, and that they did not even return the fire. Eight of our men were killed, and nine wounded. The troops then laughed, and damned the Yankees, and said they could not bear the smell of gunpowder.

Soon after this action, the troops renewed their march to Concord, where they divided into parties, and went directly to the several places where the province stores were deposited. Each party was supposed to have a Tory pilot. One body went into the jail yard, and spiked and otherwise damaged the cannon belonging to the province, and broke and set fire to the carriages. They then entered a store and rolled out about a hundred barrels of flour, which they unheaded, and emptied about forty into the river. Some took possession of the town-house, which was soon after discovered to be on fire, but which was extinguished without much damage. Another party took possession of the North Bridge. About one hundred and fifty of the militia, who had mustered upon the alarm, coming towards the bridge, were fired upon by the troops, and two were killed upon the spot. Thus did the troops of Britain's King fire FIRST at two several times upon his loyal American subjects, and put a period to ten lives before one gun was fired upon them! Our people THEN returned the fire, and obliged the troops to retreat, who were soon joined by their other parties, but finding they were still pursued, the whole body moved back to Lexington, both troops and militia firing as they went.

During this time an express was sent to General Gage, who despatched a reinforcement under the command of Earl Percy, with two field-pieces. Upon the arrival of this reinforcement at Lexington, just as the retreating party had reached there, they made a stand, picking up their dead, took all the carriages they could find, and put their wounded thereon. Others of them—to their eternal disgrace be it spoken—were robbing and setting houses on fire, and discharging their cannon at the meeting-house.

While this was transacting a party of the militia at Menotomy, attacked a party of twelve of the enemy, who were carrying stores and provision, killed one of them and took possession of their arms and stores, without any loss.

The troops having halted about an hour at Lexington, found it necessary to make a second retreat, carrying with them many of their dead and wounded. This they continued from Lexington to Charlestown, with great precipitation, the militia closely following them, firing till they reached Charlestown Neck, where they arrived a little after sunset. Passing over the Neck the enemy proceeded up Bunker Hill and encamped for the night.

INSCRIPTION ON LEXINGTON GREEN

Line of the Minute Men
April 19, 1775
Stand your ground
Don't fire unless fired upon
But if they mean to have a war
Let it begin here.

Among the natural rights of the colonists are these: First a right to life, secondly to liberty, thirdly to property; together with the right to defend them in the best manner they can.

SAMUEL ADAMS

TRIBUTE IN FANEUIL HALL, BOSTON

A few days ago I stood on the cupola of your statehouse, and overlooked for the first time this venerable city and the country surrounding it.

Then the streets, and hills, and waters around me began to teem with the life of historical recollections, recollections dear to all mankind, and a feeling of pride arose in my heart, and I said to myself, I, too, am an American citizen.

There was Bunker Hill; there Charlestown, Lexington, and Dorchester Heights not far off; there the harbor into which the British tea was sunk; there the place where the old liberty tree stood; there John Hancock's house; there Benjamin Franklin's birthplace.

And now I stand in this grand old hall, which so often resounded with the noblest appeals that ever thrilled American hearts, and where I am almost afraid to hear the echo of my own feeble voice.

No man that loves liberty, wherever he may have first seen the light of day, can fail on this sacred spot to pay his tribute to Americanism. And here, with all these glorious memories crowding upon my heart, I will offer mine.

I, born in a foreign land, pay my tribute to Americanism? Yes, for to me the word Americanism, true Americanism, comprehends the noblest ideas which ever swelled a human heart with noble pride.

CARL SCHURZ

REPORT ON THE MINUTE MEN

In the obedience to your Excellency's commands, I marched on the evening of the 18th inst. with the corps of grenadiers and light infantry for Concord, to execute your Excellency's orders with respect to destroying all ammunition, artillery, tents, &c, collected there.

I think it proper to observe, that when I had got some miles on the march from Boston, I detached six light infantry companies to march with all expedition to seize the two bridges on different roads beyond Concord. On these companies' arrival at Lexington, I understand, from the report of Major Pitcairn, who was with them, and from many officers, that they found on a green close to the road a body of the country people drawn up in military order, with arms and accoutrement, and, as appeared after, loaded.

LIEUTENANT COLONEL SMITH
TO GOVERNOR GAGE, APRIL 22, 1775

To the States or any one of them, or any city of the States, *Resist much, obey little,*
Once unquestioning obedience, once fully enslaved,
Once fully enslaved, no nation, state, city, of this earth, ever afterward resumes its liberty.

WALT WHITMAN

Under God we are determined that wheresoever, whensoever, or howsoever we shall be called to make our exit, we will die free men.

JOSIAH QUINCY

We are not to expect to be translated from despotism to liberty in a featherbed.

THOMAS JEFFERSON

"Retreat of the British from Concord,"
an early engraving from a painting by Alonzo Chappel (1820–1885)

The First Battle

The first shot of the Revolution was fired at Lexington, through which the British troops marched to Concord. There, the minutemen 450 strong, turned out to drive the Redcoats back. The early engraving is probably based on eyewitness accounts. It shows the British retreat very much as it really was.

BUNKER HILL

Here on this spot was born a nation that
will be
Adept in all the humanities. Spreading
in circles, as when
A pebble is thrown into a morning lake,
Its concepts will cover a continent with
a vision of dignity
At last made real. Here a race of men will
evolve
That will instruct the world in justice
and in love.
A race of men to whom the entire world is
a religion,
Whose vessels, laden with much more than
cargoes,
Will pass through the seven oceans, bearing
with them
The beliefs of all our countries, all our
hearts.

Let us now honor, and throughout all time,
The men who died upon this hill, the men
Who began to make us possible. The sun has
gone down again,
But it will rise tomorrow with a new
brightness,
That will be ours. O under it let us build
Our desires into events. O let us proceed
toward wisdom,
And find in ourselves the implicit order
of life,
That, swaying beneath the storms that are
always waiting to shake us,
We may still find in the lives of our heroes
the mirror of ourselves,
And see in their deaths the power of our
defenses.

HARRY PETER MCNAB BROWN, JR.

FREEDOM'S PRICE TAG

We have enjoyed so much freedom for so long that we are perhaps in danger of forgetting how much blood it cost to establish the Bill of Rights.

FELIX FRANKFURTER

From LEXINGTON

Swift as their summons came they left
The plow mid-furrow standing still,
The half-ground corn grist in the mill,
The spade in earth, the axe in cleft.

They went where duty seemed to call,
They scarcely asked the reason why;
They only knew they could but die,
And death was not the worst of all!

Of man for man the sacrifice,
All that was theirs to give, they gave.
The flowers that blossomed from their
grave
Have sown themselves beneath all skies.

JOHN GREENLEAF WHITTIER

It is in vain, sir, to extenuate the matter. Gentlemen may cry, Peace, peace; but there is no peace. The war is actually begun. The next gale that sweeps from the North will bring to our ears the clash of resounding arms. Our brethren are already in the field. Why stand we here idle? What is it that gentlemen wish? What would they have? Is life so dear, or peace so sweet, as to be purchased at the price of chains and slavery? Forbid it, Almighty God!—I know not what course others may take; but as for me, give me liberty or give me death!

—Patrick Henry

These are the times that try men's souls. The summer soldier and the sunshine patriot will in this crisis shrink from the service of his country; but he that stands it NOW, deserves the love and thanks of man and woman. Tyranny, like hell, is not easily conquered; yet we have this consolation with us, that the harder the conflict, the more glorious the triumph. What we obtain too cheap, we esteem too lightly; 't is dearness only that gives everything its value. Heaven knows how to put a proper price upon its goods; and it would be strange indeed, if so celestial an article as FREEDOM should not be highly rated.

—Thomas Paine, in "The Crisis"

The news of Lexington spread rapidly, strengthening everywhere the spirit of revolt. In Vermont Ethan Allen on his own initiative raised a company of "Green Mountain Boys" and captured Ticonderoga, May 10, 1775, and Crown Point two days later. A gathering of militiamen in Mecklenburg County, North Carolina, declared the existing civil and military commissions null and void, and established a local government "until laws shall be provided for us by the Congress"—an action that was virtually a declaration of independence. In the meantime the siege of Boston was pushed vigorously. To oust the British it would be necessary to occupy and hold the heights behind Boston, either at Charlestown or at Dorchester, and, on the night of June 16, Colonel Prescott occupied Breed's Hill in Charlestown.[1] Against the bombardment of the British fleet the colonials held their position throughout the morning of the June 17. In the afternoon Gage ordered Sir William Howe to storm the position. Twice the British regulars advanced only to be driven back by the withering fire of the militia. On the third attempt the Americans, their ammunition exhausted, retreated. The British held Breed's Hill, which enabled them to remain in Boston, but their loss of over 1000 killed or wounded was so severe and the fighting qualities displayed by the American militia so great that the colonials considered the battle as good as a victory.

On the day that Ethan Allen captured the fortress of Ticonderoga the second Continental Congress met at Philadelphia. Its powers, if it had any, were extremely vague; it represented, said Bancroft, "nothing more than the unformed opinion of an unformed people." But no abler group of representatives has probably ever assembled on the American continent, and, confronted by a war actually existing, they speedily took charge of the situation. On the request of Massachusetts they assumed responsibility for the troops around Boston, appointed George Washington as commander-in-chief of the continental army, and authorized an expedition against Canada. Massachusetts and New Hampshire, asking for advice respecting the formation of a new government, were urged to proceed "until a governor of his Majesty's appointment shall consent to govern the province according to its charter." From the pens of John Dickinson and Thomas Jefferson came a stirring Declaration of the Causes and Necessity of Taking up Arms, and upon the advice of Dickinson another petition was addressed to the king.

Despite the actions of the Congress and the fact that war actually existed, independence, except in the minds of the extreme radicals, seemed far from the thoughts of the delegates. "We have not raised armies with ambitious designs of separating from Great Britain, and establishing independent states," said the Declaration of Causes, and this must be accepted as sober truth. "It is well known," said Jefferson in 1782, "that in July, 1775, a separation from Great Britain and the establishment of a Republican Government had not yet entered any person's mind." As late as the autumn of that year the legislatures of at least five states were on record against independence, and in January, 1776, the king's health was still being toasted at the officer's mess presided over by Washington. Whatever may have been the feeling of the majority of the delegates, events had gone too far for an amicable settlement. The king refused to receive the petition addressed to him by Congress. In August he issued a proclamation declaring the colonies in a state of rebellion, and in September he hired 20,000 Hessians to put down the revolt. During the following month the British navy, without provocation, burned Falmouth Harbor (Portland, Maine), and in January it burned Norfolk, Virginia. On December 22, 1775, an act of Parliament forbade all trade and intercourse with the colonies. "It throws thirteen colonies out of the royal protection," said John Adams when he received news of this act, "and makes us independent in spite of supplications and entreaties."

He was right. Both sides had gone too far to turn back.

The Birth of A Nation

"The Declaration of Independence" by John Trumbull (1756–1843), who served in the Revolution and knew its leaders.

IN CONGRESS, July 4, 1776.

The unanimous Declaration of the thirteen united States of America,

When in the Course of human events, it becomes necessary for one people to dissolve the political bands which have connected them with another, and to assume among the powers of the earth, the separate and equal station to which the Laws of Nature and of Nature's God entitle them, a decent respect to the opinions of mankind requires that they should declare the causes which impel them to the separation. —— We hold these truths to be self-evident, that all men are created equal, that they are endowed by their Creator with certain unalienable Rights, that among these are Life, Liberty and the pursuit of Happiness. — That to secure these rights, Governments are instituted among Men, deriving their just powers from the consent of the governed, — That whenever any Form of Government becomes destructive of these ends, it is the Right of the People to alter or to abolish it, and to institute new Government, laying its foundation on such principles and organizing its powers in such form, as to them shall seem most likely to effect their Safety and Happiness. Prudence, indeed, will dictate that Governments long established should not be changed for light and transient causes; and accordingly all experience hath shewn, that mankind are more disposed to suffer, while evils are sufferable, than to right themselves by abolishing the forms to which they are accustomed. But when a long train of abuses and usurpations, pursuing invariably the same Object evinces a design to reduce them under absolute Despotism, it is their right, it is their duty, to throw off such Government, and to provide new Guards for their future security. — Such has been the patient sufferance of these Colonies; and such is now the necessity which constrains them to alter their former Systems of Government. The history of the present King of Great Britain is a history of repeated injuries and usurpations, all having in direct object the establishment of an absolute Tyranny over these States. To prove this, let Facts be submitted to a candid world. —— He has refused his Assent to Laws, the most wholesome and necessary for the public good. —— He has forbidden his Governors to pass Laws of immediate and pressing importance, unless suspended in their operation till his Assent should be obtained; and when so suspended, he has utterly neglected to attend to them. —— He has refused to pass other Laws for the accommodation of large districts of people, unless those people would relinquish the right of Representation in the Legislature, a right inestimable to them and formidable to tyrants only. —— He has called together legislative bodies at places unusual, uncomfortable, and distant from the depository of their Public Records, for the sole purpose of fatiguing them into compliance with his measures. —— He has dissolved Representative Houses repeatedly, for opposing with manly firmness his invasions on the rights of the people. —— He has refused for a long time, after such dissolutions, to cause others to be elected; whereby the Legislative powers, incapable of Annihilation, have returned to the People at large for their exercise; the State remaining in the mean time exposed to all the dangers of invasion from without, and convulsions within. —— He has endeavoured to prevent the population of these States; for that purpose obstructing the Laws for Naturalization of Foreigners; refusing to pass others to encourage their migrations hither, and raising the conditions of new Appropriations of Lands. —— He has obstructed the Administration of Justice, by refusing his Assent to Laws for establishing Judiciary powers. —— He has made Judges dependent on his Will alone, for the tenure of their offices, and the amount and payment of their salaries. —— He has erected a multitude of New Offices, and sent hither swarms of Officers to harrass our people, and eat out their substance. —— He has kept among us, in times of peace, Standing Armies without the Consent of our legislatures. —— He has affected to render the Military independent of and superior to the Civil power. —— He has combined with others to subject us to a jurisdiction foreign to our constitution, and unacknowledged by our laws; giving his Assent to their Acts of pretended Legislation: — For Quartering large bodies of armed troops among us: — For protecting them, by a mock Trial, from punishment for any Murders which they should commit on the Inhabitants of these States: — For cutting off our Trade with all parts of the world: — For imposing Taxes on us without our Consent: — For depriving us in many cases, of the benefits of Trial by Jury: — For transporting us beyond Seas to be tried for pretended offences: — For abolishing the free System of English Laws in a neighbouring Province, establishing therein an Arbitrary government, and enlarging its Boundaries so as to render it at once an example and fit instrument for introducing the same absolute rule into these Colonies: — For taking away our Charters, abolishing our most valuable Laws, and altering fundamentally the Forms of our Governments: — For suspending our own Legislatures, and declaring themselves invested with power to legislate for us in all cases whatsoever. — He has abdicated Government here, by declaring us out of his Protection and waging War against us. —— He has plundered our seas, ravaged our Coasts, burnt our towns, and destroyed the lives of our people. —— He is at this time transporting large Armies of foreign Mercenaries to compleat the works of death, desolation and tyranny, already begun with circumstances of Cruelty & perfidy scarcely paralleled in the most barbarous ages, and totally unworthy the Head of a civilized nation. —— He has constrained our fellow Citizens taken Captive on the high Seas to bear Arms against their Country, to become the executioners of their friends and Brethren, or to fall themselves by their Hands. —— He has excited domestic insurrections amongst us, and has endeavoured to bring on the inhabitants of our frontiers, the merciless Indian Savages, whose known rule of warfare, is an undistinguished destruction of all ages, sexes and conditions. In every stage of these Oppressions We have Petitioned for Redress in the most humble terms: Our repeated Petitions have been answered only by repeated injury. A Prince, whose character is thus marked by every act which may define a Tyrant, is unfit to be the ruler of a free people. Nor have We been wanting in attentions to our Brittish brethren. We have warned them from time to time of attempts by their legislature to extend an unwarrantable jurisdiction over us. We have reminded them of the circumstances of our emigration and settlement here. We have appealed to their native justice and magnanimity, and we have conjured them by the ties of our common kindred to disavow these usurpations, which, would inevitably interrupt our connections and correspondence. They too have been deaf to the voice of justice and of consanguinity. We must, therefore, acquiesce in the necessity, which denounces our Separation, and hold them, as we hold the rest of mankind, Enemies in War, in Peace Friends. ——

We, therefore, the Representatives of the united States of America, in General Congress, Assembled, appealing to the Supreme Judge of the world for the rectitude of our intentions, do, in the Name, and by Authority of the good People of these Colonies, solemnly publish and declare, That these United Colonies are, and of Right ought to be Free and Independent States; that they are Absolved from all Allegiance to the British Crown, and that all political connection between them and the State of Great Britain, is and ought to be totally dissolved; and that as Free and Independent States, they have full Power to levy War, conclude Peace, contract Alliances, establish Commerce, and to do all other Acts and Things which Independent States may of right do. —— And for the support of this Declaration, with a firm reliance on the protection of divine Providence, we mutually pledge to each other our Lives, our Fortunes and our sacred Honor.

John Hancock

Button Gwinnett
Lyman Hall
Geo Walton.

Wm Hooper
Joseph Hewes,
John Penn

Edward Rutledge 1.

Thos Heyward Junr.
Thomas Lynch Junr.
Arthur Middleton

Samuel Chase
Wm Paca
Thos Stone
Charles Carroll of Carrollton

George Wythe
Richard Henry Lee
Th Jefferson
Benja Harrison
Thos Nelson jr.
Francis Lightfoot Lee
Carter Braxton

Robt Morris
Benjamin Rush
Benja Franklin
John Morton
Geo Clymer
Jas Smith
Geo. Taylor
James Wilson
Geo. Ross

Caesar Rodney
Geo Read
Tho M:Kean

Wm Floyd
Phil. Livingston
Frans Lewis
Lewis Morris

Richd Stockton
Jno Witherspoon
Fras Hopkinson
John Hart
Abra Clark

Josiah Bartlett
Wm Whipple
Saml Adams
John Adams
Robt Treat Paine
Elbridge Gerry
Step Hopkins
William Ellery
Roger Sherman
Saml Huntington
Wm Williams
Oliver Wolcott
Matthew Thornton

Signers of the Declaration of Independence

New Hampshire

Josiah Bartlett, 1729–1795
Matthew Thornton, 1714(?)–1803
William Whipple, 1730–1785

Massachusetts

John Adams, 1735–1826
Samuel Adams, 1722–1803
Elbridge Gerry, 1744–1814
John Hancock, 1737–1793
Robert Treat Paine, 1731–1814

Rhode Island

William Ellery, 1727–1820
Stephen Hopkins, 1707–1785

Connecticut

Samuel Huntington, 1731–1796
Roger Sherman, 1721–1793
William Williams, 1731–1811
Oliver Wolcott, 1726–1797

New York

William Floyd, 1734–1821
Francis Lewis, 1713–1803
Philip Livingston, 1716–1778
Lewis Morris, 1726–1798

New Jersey

Abraham Clark, 1726–1794
John Hart, 1711(?)–1779
Francis Hopkinson, 1737–1791
Richard Stockton, 1730–1781
John Witherspoon, 1723–1794

Maryland

Charles Carroll, 1737–1832
Samuel Chase, 1741–1811
William Paca, 1740–1799
Thomas Stone, 1743–1787

Delaware

Thomas McKean, 1734–1817
George Read, 1733–1798
Caesar Rodney, 1728–1784

Pennsylvania

George Clymer, 1739–1813
Benjamin Franklin, 1706–1790
Robert Morris, 1734–1806
John Morton, 1724(?)–1777
George Ross, 1730–1779
Benjamin Rush, 1745(?)–1813
James Smith, 1719(?)–1806
George Taylor, 1716–1781
James Wilson, 1742–1798

Virginia

Carter Braxton, 1736–1797
Benjamin Harrison, 1726(?)–1791
Thomas Jefferson, 1743–1826
Francis Lightfoot Lee, 1734–1797
Richard Henry Lee, 1732–1794
Thomas Nelson, Jr., 1738–1789
George Wythe, 1726–1806

North Carolina

Joseph Hewes, 1730–1779
William Hooper, 1742–1790
John Penn, 1741(?)–1788

South Carolina

Thomas Heyward, Jr., 1746–1809
Thomas Lynch, Jr., 1749–1779
Arthur Middleton, 1742–1787
Edward Rutledge, 1749–1800

Georgia

Button Gwinnett, 1735(?)–1777
Lyman Hall, 1724(?)–1790
George Walton, 1741(?)–1804

Birth of a Nation

On June 7, 1776, Richard Henry Lee, who had issued the first call for a congress of the colonies, introduced in the Continental Congress at Philadelphia a resolution declaring "that these united Colonies are, and of right ought to be, free and independent states, that they are absolved from all allegiance to the British Crown, and that all political connection between them and the state of Great Britain is, and ought to be, totally dissolved."

The resolution, seconded by John Adams on behalf of the Massachusetts delegation, came up again June 10 when a committee of five, headed by Thomas Jefferson, was appointed to express the purpose of the resolution in a declaration of independence. The others on the committee were John Adams, Benjamin Franklin, Robert R. Livingston and Roger Sherman.

Drafting the Declaration was assigned to Jefferson, who worked on a portable desk of his own construction in a room at Market and 7th streets in Philadelphia. The committee reported the result June 28, 1776. The members of the Congress suggested a number of changes, which Jefferson called "deplorable." They didn't approve Jefferson's arraignment of the British people and King George III for encouraging and fostering the slave trade, which Jefferson called "an execrable commerce." They made 86 changes, eliminating 480 words and leaving 1,337. In the final form capitalization was erratic. Jefferson had written that men were endowed with "inalienable" rights; in the final copy it came out as "unalienable" and has been thus ever since.

The Lee-Adams resolution of independence was adopted by 12 yeas July 2—the actual date of the act of independence. The Declaration, which explains the act, was adopted July 4.

After the Declaration was adopted July 4, 1776, it was turned over to John Dunlap, printer, to be printed on broadsides. The original copy was lost and one of his broadsides was attached to a page in the journal of the Congress. It was read aloud July 8 in Philadelphia, Easton, Pa. and Trenton, N. J. On July 9 at 6 p.m., it was read by order of Gen. George Washington to the troops assembled on the Common in New York City.

The Continental Congress on July 19, 1776 adopted the following resolution:

"Resolved, That the Declaration passed on the 4th, be fairly engrossed on parchment with the title and stile of The unanimous Declaration of the thirteen united States of America and that the same, when engrossed, be signed by every member of Congress."

Not all delegates who signed the engrossed Declaration were present on July 4. Robert Morris (Pa.), William Williams (Conn.) and Samuel Chase (Md.) signed on Aug. 2. Oliver Wolcott (Conn.), George Wythe (Va.), Richard Henry Lee (Va.) and Elbridge Gerry (Mass.) signed in August and September. Matthew Thornton (N.H.) joined the Congress Nov. 4 and signed later. Thomas McKean (Del.) rejoined Washington's Army before signing and said later that he signed in 1781.

INDEPENDENCE HALL.

Charles Carroll of Carrollton was appointed a delegate by Maryland on July 4, 1776, presented his credentials July 18, and signed the engrossed Declaration Aug. 2. Born Sept. 19, 1737, he was 95 years old and the last surviving signer when he died Nov. 14, 1832.

Two Pennsylvania delegates who did not support the Declaration on July 4 were replaced.

The four New York delegates did not have authority from their state to vote on July 4. On July 9, the New York state convention authorized its delegates to approve the Declaration and the Congress was so notified on July 15, 1776. The four signed the engrossed Declaration on Aug. 2.

The original engrossed Declaration is preserved in the National Archives Building in Washington, D. C.

Let them know that while every colony honors the mother city so long as it is well treated, yet that if wronged, it becomes alienated; for colonists are not sent out to be slaves of those who are left behind, but to be their equals.

THUCYDIDES

They Endured For Us

Washington's army was continually in need of food, clothing, munitions, and medicines; Valley Forge was only the most spectacular episode in over six years of suffering due to inadequate popular support. As late as 1782 General Greene declared, "Our men are almost naked for want of overalls and sheets and the greater part of the army barefoot." Nor was it all the fault of Congress, which did everything possible to finance the war. As always in time of war, there were many who were quite willing to profit from the public need. "Such a dearth of public spirit," said Washington in 1775, "and want of virtue, such stock-jobbing and fertility in all the low arts to obtain advantage of one kind or another . . . I never saw before, and I pray God I may never be a witness to again. . . . Such a dirty mercenary spirit pervades the whole that I should not be at all surprised at any disaster that may happen."

Under such circumstances it is not surprising that the number of soldiers, militia and regulars, in the American army was always small in comparison to the man power of the country.[1] Only upon exceptional occasions did the total American forces reach thirty or forty thousand. Including the sick and ineffectives, Washington never had more than 16,000 in the summer of 1776, and just before Trenton his force had sunk to but 5000. There were times when he could barely put two or three thousand in the field. The majority of the American forces were always militia, and for these Washington had almost as much contempt as the British, a feeling that was far from being justified, for these same militia had given a good account of themselves at Bunker Hill, Saratoga, and many another critical battle in the Revolution. In letters to Congress Washington frequently complained of his "want of confidence in the generality of the troops" and of the militia that they "come in, you cannot tell how; go, you cannot tell when, and act you cannot tell where, consume your provisions, exhaust your stores, and leave you at last at a critical moment."

[1]"Taking the highest estimate of three million as the total population of the continental colonies in 1775," says Professor Channing, "and regarding forty per cent as military revolutionists, this would be twelve hundred thousand, of whom one-fifth would be men of military age, or two hundred and fifty thousand at the outside." *History of the United States,* III, 221.

One man with courage makes a majority.

ANDREW JACKSON

VALLEY FORGE.

Washington and Lafayette visiting the suffering army.

Reason and experience both forbid us to expect that national morality can prevail in exclusion of religious principles.

GEORGE WASHINGTON

TOMB OF THE UNKNOWN REVOLUTIONARY SOLDIER

Here lies a soldier of
The Revolution whose identity
Is known but to God.
His was an idealism
That recognized a Supreme
Being, that planted
Religious liberty on our
Shores, that overthrew
Despotism, that established
A people's government,
That wrote a Constitution
Setting metes and bounds
Of delegated authority,
That fixed a standard of
Value upon men above
Gold and lifted high the
Torch of civil liberty
Along the pathway of
Mankind.
In ourselves his soul
Exists as part of ours,
His memory's mansion.

ALEXANDRIA, VIRGINIA

(WRITTEN BY WILLIAM TYLER PAGE)

"Our Lives, Our Fortunes"

With the invading fleet already at their shores, the four New York delegates—Francis Lewis, William Floyd, Philip Livingston, and Lewis Morris—practically signed away their property when they put their names to the Declaration. This they knew, and they also felt the gravest concern for their families. These men were wealthy aristocrats, with luxurious town houses and country estates filled with attractive loot for plundering.

The conquering army swarmed over Long Island. They burned and plundered the home of Signer Francis Lewis at Whitestone, and carried off his wife as a prisoner. Mrs. Lewis was confined in a filthy barracks and treated with great brutality. She had no bed to lie on, and no change of clothing for months. This disgraceful treatment came to the attention of Congress. General Washington then arranged for her exchange for two women prisoners of the Americans.

Mrs. Lewis had suffered so severely that she never regained her health, and died two years later.

William Floyd was practically ruined by the Revolution. His home and lands were taken over and spoiled by the Tories. Mrs. Floyd and their children escaped to Connecticut. They were exiled from their home for seven years.

Philip Livingston's business interests and mansion, plus his country estate fell to the enemy. His family fled, and he never returned home, he died in 1778.

Lewis Morris and family suffered the loss of home and lands for seven years. He had three sons who served as officers in the American army.

The five New Jersey signers were hounded by the Tories, British and Hessian soldiers. "Honest John" Hart had a large farm and several mills. While his wife lay on her deathbed, Hessian soldiers descended upon his place, devastating his lands and destroying his mills. Hart fled and was hunted like a wild animal. By the time he (a broken man at 65) could return, his wife had died and his thirteen children scattered in every direction.

Abraham Clark had two sons in the army who were captured by the British and treated harshly because of their father's patriotism.

Judge Richard Stockton, father-in-law of Dr. Benjamin Rush, his home and fortune in Tory hands, was thrown in prison. Invalided by harsh treatment in prison (a shocked Congress arranged for his parole) he lost life and fortune.

Francis Hopkinson's home was ransacked by the British.

The Pennsylvania signers suffered as follows: George Clymer lost his home and the furnishings were looted, after his family was forced to flee.

Dr. Benjamin Rush's home was taken over for headquarters of British General Howe. He was an army doctor and narrowly escaped capture after the Battle of Brandywine.

James Smith lost his large fortune.

George Taylor suffered great financial loss.

John Morton was the first of all the Signers to die, April 1777. His last words were, "Tell them they will live to see the hour when they shall acknowledge it to have been the most glorious service that I ever rendered to my country."

Robert Morris, the financial genius for General Washington and the Revolution, lost most of his huge shipping business.

William Ellery (Rhode Island) pledged a large fortune, which he lost within a few months to the cause. The British burned his home and destroyed all of his property.

Edward Rutledge (South Carolina), at twenty-six was the youngest signer. Benjamin Franklin (Pennsylvania) was the oldest, at seventy.

The three other Signers from South Carolina, Arthur Middleton, Thomas Heyward, Jr., and Thomas Lynch, Jr., all saw military service and were captured and imprisoned.

George Walton (Georgia) was badly wounded, captured and imprisoned when the British captured Savannah.

The enemy destroyed the home of Lyman Hall (Georgia) and devastated his rice plantation.

Thomas Nelson, Jr. (Virginia) had raised a necessary $2,000,000 for the Revolution, almost overnight by putting up his own properties as collateral. They were forfeited when the loans came due; his government never reimbursed him. Health and wealth gone, he died in modest circumstances, at age fifty.

Carter Braxton, (Virginia) lost his fortune in ships, to the enemy, and spent the rest of his life in poverty.

Maryland's Charles Carroll outlived by six years the last of the other Signers, dying in 1832 at the age of ninety-five.

Democracy is based upon the conviction that there are extraordinary possibilities in ordinary people.

HARRY EMERSON FOSDICK

MEMORIAL TABLET

General Charles Cotesworth Pinckney
One of the founders of
the American Republic.
In war
he was the companion in arms
and the friend of Washington.
In peace
he enjoyed his unchanging confidence
and maintained with enlightened zeal
the principles of his administration
and of the Constitution.
As a Statesman
he bequeathed to his country the sentiment,
Millions for defence
Not a cent for tribute.
As a lawyer
his learning was various and profound,
his principles pure, his practice liberal.
With all the accomplishments
of the gentleman
he combined the virtues of the patriot
and the piety of the Christian.
His name
is recorded in the history of his country
inscribed on the charter of her liberties
and cherished in the affections of her
citizens.

SAINT MICHAEL'S CHURCH
CHARLESTON, SOUTH CAROLINA

ALTAR AT VALLEY FORGE

The sublimest figure in American history is Washington on his knees at Valley Forge.

He was in that hour and place the American personified, not depending on their own courage or goodness, but asking aid from God, their Father and Preserver.

Washington knew that morals are priceless, but he knew that morals are from within. And he knew that in that dread day when all, save courage, had forsaken the American arms, appeal must be to that Power beyond ourselves, eternal in the heavens, which after all, in every crisis of the lives of men and nations, has been their surest source of strength.

ALBERT J. BEVERIDGE

Centennial Ode, July 4, 1876

God of our fathers, thou who wast,
Art, and shalt be when those eye-wise who
flout
Thy secret presence shall be lost
In the great light that dazzles them to
doubt,
We, sprung from loins of stalwart men
Whose strength was in their trust
That thou wouldst make thy dwelling in their
dust
And walk with those a fellow-citizen
Who build a city of the just,
We, who believe Life's bases rest
Beyond the probe of chemic test,
Still, like our fathers, feel thee near,
Sure that, while lasts the immutable decree,
The land to Human Nature dear
Shall not be unbeloved of thee.

JAMES RUSSELL LOWELL

A SIGNER DECLARES

There is a tide in the affairs of men, a nick of time. We perceive it now before us. To hesitate is to consent to our own slavery.

That noble instrument upon your table, that insures immortality to its author, should be subscribed this very morning by every pen in this house. He that will not respond to its accents, and strain every nerve to carry into effect its provisions, is unworthy of the name of free man.

For my own part, of property, I have some; of reputation, more. That reputation is staked, that property is pledged on the issue of this contest; and although these grey hairs must soon descend into the sepulcher, I would infinitely rather that they descend thither by the hand of the executioner than desert at this crisis the sacred cause of my country.

JOHN WITHERSPOON

Sacred Hall of Independence

Here, on July 4, 1776, was adopted the Declaration, from which flow all the blessings of our life and land

Condensed from The Denver Post
PAUL FRIGGENS

Some time ago guards at Independence Hall in Philadelphia noticed that a graying, shabby little woman came in frequently to visit this national shrine. Then they discovered that on occasion she would leave a dollar bill beside the Liberty Bell. Questioned, the refugee from an Iron Curtain country explained in halting English, "Now I know what freedom mean to me, I give something back."

Every year more than 1,500,000 visitors, including 50,000 from abroad, make their pilgrimage to this spot marked simply by a tablet at the entrance: "Birthplace of the United States of America." A Wyoming ranch family, driving through Philadelphia late one night, wanted to see the shrine and asked a policeman for directions. After dark the Liberty Bell is spotlighted through glass-paneled doors, and the Wyoming couple and their youngsters stood in rapture. "They'd come so far that I opened the doors and let them in to touch the Bell," says guard Joe Ostrowski. Equally inspired was a blind war veteran, as his wife guided his fingers over the raised inscription on the Bell: "Proclaim LIBERTY throughout all the Land, unto all the Inhabitants thereof."

Today Independence Hall has come to symbolize the rights of free men everywhere. "Ah, the Bell!" Premier David Ben-Gurion of Israel cried, and started to examine it. He stopped short. "But am I worthy to touch it?"

Historian Carl Van Doren points out that in Independence Hall the United States was "created" on July 4, 1776, with the framing of the Declaration of Independence, and "perpetuated" on September 17, 1787, with the adoption of our Constitution. Here also we created a Continental Army and Navy, adopted the Stars and Stripes as our nation's flag and established the temporary capital of the United States.

In recent years Independence Hall was run-down and surrounded by slums. Now an eight-block jungle of firetraps and dilapidated shops has been razed to give it a dignified setting in a new Independence National Historical Park. Some 110 structures in the federal park, including a ten-story office building, have already been leveled in a bold 30-million-dollar project first sparked by civic and patriotic organizations banded together as the Independence Hall Association. The park will preserve perhaps a score of other treasured buildings and sites in "America's most historic square mile." Eventually the shrine will be fully restored, with imposing mall, brick walls, wrought-iron fences and serpentine, shaded walks as in the late 18th century.

The Liberty Bell

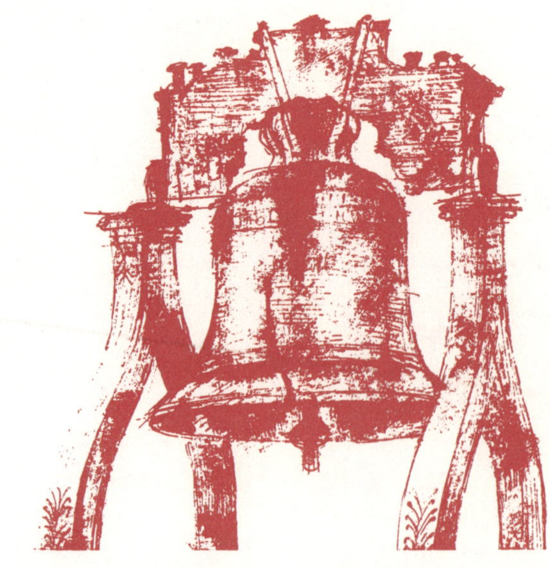

The noble old two-story Georgian building, erected between 1732 and 1753 as the Pennsylvania State House, is commencing to look fresh and prideful again. The National Park Service has peeled off some 60 coats of paint in places, and is carefully investigating the fabric and physical history of the edifice. Its researchers have pored over musty records here and abroad to piece together all that happened in this stately building. "There's no more stirring story," says park superintendent Melford O. Anderson, "and Americans ought to know it better."

Step into the historic Assembly Room with its high Colonial windows, twin fireplaces, green-covered desks and quill pens, together with the commanding portrait of George Washington by Charles Willson Peale, and the American Revolution comes alive again.

The Revolution, said John Adams, occurred in "the minds and hearts of the people." King George III and his ministers provoked the people with harsh customs regulations and a stamp tax on everything from newspapers to playing cards. The crowning blow came with the British Parliament's insistence on legislating for the Colonies "in all cases whatsoever."

In September 1774, 12 of the 13 Colonies dispatched delegations of leading citizens to an assembly in Philadelphia to seek redress for their grievances. (Georgia did not participate until the next year.) Philadelphia was then a "greene towne" on the edge of the wilderness. It was plagued by insufferable summer heat, horseflies and the dread yellow fever, but it boasted 35,000 inhabitants, cobbled streets, a thriving commerce and culture. It was to become the center of American resistance.

From their hostels the delegates walked to Carpenters' Hall for their first meeting as the Continental Congress. They adopted a manifesto of grievances, pledged support to the beleaguered people of Boston, embargoed British goods and petitioned the king to restore the "rights of Englishmen."

The following spring, on April 19, 1775, the thin line of embattled Minutemen at Lexington and Concord stood fast against a detachment of redcoats sent to seize some military stores, and the Second Continental Congress convened under a cloud of war. Gathering for the first time in the State House, Congress chose George Washington as general and commander in chief of the ragtag Continental Army, and addressed a final olive-branch appeal to Britain.

The Revolution took a decisive turn on June 7, 1776. On instructions from his Virginia Convention, Richard Henry Lee rose in the State House to propose a dramatic resolution: *"That these United Colonies are, and of right ought to be, free and independent States."* The resolution loosed a torrent of debate.

After days of bitter argument delegates favoring independence won out, and a five-man committee, including Benjamin Franklin and John Adams, was selected to draft a declaration "setting forth the causes which impelled us to this mighty resolution." One of its members, 33-year-old Thomas Jefferson, was asked to write the document. So this lanky, redheaded Virginian toiled between June 11 and June 28 in a second-floor room of a German bricklayer's house, penning the finest statement of democratic principles in all history.

On July 3, Jefferson slipped into a rear seat in the Assembly Room and listened while Congress took up his draft of the Declaration. Written in Jefferson's neat, clear hand, it was an eloquent series of charges against the Crown, but what breathed eternal fire into it and stirred the Congress was this passage: *"We hold these truths to be self-evident, that all men are created equal, that they are endowed by their Creator with certain unalienable Rights, that among these are Life, Liberty and the pursuit of Happiness."* And again, the immutable principle that government derives its powers *"from the consent of the governed."* This is the heart of American democracy.

Congress spent nearly two days pruning and editing the document. But in the end the lofty sentiment, timeless philosophy and cadenced phrasing of the Declaration remained almost wholly Jefferson's—and wholly American. John Adams called it "the very essence of the American mind." It was afternoon, July 4, when Congress, mutually pledging *"our Lives, our Fortunes, and our sacred Honour,"* unanimously adopted the Declaration, ordering it to be published and proclaimed.

Legend has it that on July 4, 1776, an old bellman stood in the steeple of Independence Hall, eagerly awaiting the signal from a boy stationed at the Assembly Room door. As the Congress jubilantly approved the Declaration, the boy shouted, "Ring, Grandfather, ring!" And so, it is said, our liberty was first proclaimed to the world.

Today, on rare state occasions, the Liberty Bell is tapped with a rubber mallet, and its muted tone has been recorded for posterity. But its real message is symbolic. As the guides tell tens of thousands of visitors to Independence Hall, "The Liberty Bell reminds each of us not only of our rights and privileges but also of our duties and responsibilities."

On July 4, 1826, the 50th anniversary of the signing of the Declaration of Independence, Thomas Jefferson and John Adams died within a few minutes of each other—first, 83-year-old Jefferson, at Monticello; then, in Quincy, Mass., hardy John Adams, at 91. Shortly before, when a group of citizens asked Adams for a watchword for the 50th-anniversary celebration, he had offered a toast that is meaningful to all liberty-loving people. "I give you," said the old patriot, "INDEPENDENCE FOREVER!"

UNQUENCHABLE FAITH

On the Fourth of July, 1826, America celebrated its Jubilee—the Fiftieth Anniversary of Independence. John Adams, second President of the United States, died that day, aged ninety, while from Maine to Georgia bells rang and cannon boomed. And on that same day, Thomas Jefferson died before sunset in Virginia.

In their dying, in that swift, so aptly celebrated double departure, is something which shakes an American to the heart. It was not their great fame, their long lives or even the record of their work that made these two seem indestructible. It was their faith, their bounding, unquenchable faith in the future, their sure, immortal belief that mankind, if it so desired, could be free.

CATHERINE DRINKER BOWEN

NATHAN HALE

I only regret that I have but one life to lose for my country.

NATHAN HALE (September 22, 1776)

Far dearer, the grave or the prison,
Illumed by one patriot name,
Than the trophies of all who have risen
On Liberty's ruins to fame.

—*Thomas Moore*

No man is worth his salt who is not ready at all times to risk his body, to risk his well-being, to risk his life, in a great cause.—Theodore Roosevelt.

A Giant of the Revolution

By Nancy Hale

Nathan Hale was only a couple of years out of New Haven when he joined up. He'd hardly got started. He'd been teaching school, you know, up at East Haddam and then down in New London, and it looked as if he was shaping up into a fine teacher. He'd made a lot of friends everywhere he went, and the girls always liked him. They say he was a good-looking boy.

Then the war came. Things had looked bad to Americans for a long time, but when the first gun was fired on that April day it seemed to light a sudden, strong fire in everyone's heart. It seemed to call out—"Americans!" The boy's brothers, John and Joseph, volunteered first off. It was a patriotic family—the father had been a deputy in the old Connecticut Assembly.

The boy himself had signed up with the school for a year. He wasn't the kind to let people down, but he did write and ask to be released from his contract two weeks early. He joined up in July, as a lieutenant in Webb's Seventh Connecticut.

Well, you know how things went after that. The boy was in camp near Boston all Winter. It wasn't an exciting siege. But there was a lot to do getting the men to re-enlist. Most of their terms of enlistment ran out in December. General Washington was worried about it. Our boy offered the men in his company his own pay for a month if they'd stay longer. Anyway, the siege was maintained.

He got a leave in the Winter and went home. Maybe that was when he got engaged—to Alicia Adams. A lovely girl; they would have made a handsome couple.

When Spring came, the enemy evacuated Boston and the American army went down to New York, where real trouble was threatening. The boy had been made a captain by that time. He was 21 years old.

Our Long Island campaign was just this side of disastrous. Morale was none too good, afterward. I don't suppose the general was in a worse spot in the whole war than he was for those three weeks right after the Battle of Long Island.

There we lay, facing the enemy across the East River, and no way of knowing what they had up their sleeve. Surprise was what we feared. The answer to that was companies of rangers, to scout around and find what was up. Knowlton's Rangers were organized, and our boy got switched over to them. He wanted action, you see.

But the Rangers weren't enough. The general wanted to know two things: when the enemy was planning to attack, and where. Nobody could tell him. The general let it be known that he'd welcome volunteers to spy.

Now people didn't take kindly to the word "spy" around these parts. It didn't mean excitement or glamour or any of those things. It meant something degrading. But the general said he wanted a spy. Well, our boy volunteered. His friends tried to talk him out of it. They spoke of the indignity; they also told him he'd make a terrible spy—a frank, fine boy like him.

But to him the task was necessary. Its being necessary seemed to him to make it honorable. He was sent through the enemy lines dressed like a Dutch schoolmaster.

He didn't make such a bad spy after all. He got what he went after. In his shoes he hid drawings that would have been valuable to our army. He was on his way back, crossing their lines, when he was caught.

The British found the information on him. He admitted he was a spy. You know what a spy gets. They hanged him the next morning.

He wrote some letters to the family at home. They were destroyed before his eyes, they say. But, in his last moment, they let him say what he wanted to. And later one of their officers told one of our officers what he'd said.

There he was, at Turtle Bay on Manhattan Island, with the noose around his neck. He'd got caught on his first big job. He wasn't going to get to marry Alicia Adams, nor do any more teaching, nor finish fighting this war. He stood there in the morning air, and told them who he was, his rank and all. And then he added, "I only regret that I have but one life to lose for my country."

You could tell the story like that, because it is a simple story, and when you'd finished you'd have told about all there is to tell about Nathan Hale. There isn't even a contemporary picture of him. Most of the friends to whom he wrote didn't keep his letters. He was just a young American who'd gone to war, who'd lived for 21 uneventful years before he died for his country.

One of his brothers, Enoch, was my great-great-grandfather.

When I was a child a small bronze statue, about four feet high, stood in the corner of the living room at home. It was that of a young man, with his wrists tied behind him and his ankles bound. I passed it several times a day, every day of my childhood. Sometimes I used to touch the bronze face. It was a small-scale replica of the Nathan Hale statue at Yale.

I must have been told his story, because I always knew it. But my father never went on about it, if you know what I mean. There his story was; for what it might mean to you. Some of my other ancestors were the kind of characters that have a whole legend of anecdotes surrounding them, stirring, or uproarious. But the young man with his hands bound had died at 21, a patriot, as stark and all alone and anecdoteless as young men of 21 must be.

Once I was set upon the knees of an old gentleman whose grandmother was Alicia Adams. She had married and had children, and lived to be 88, a pretty, sparkling old lady. And when she died she said, "Where is Nathan?" But about the young man himself there were no family reminiscences, no old little jokes, no tales beyond the short, plain story of his life and death. He had had no time to do anything memorable but die.

Nevertheless. . . . it was my job as a child to fill the kitchen scuttle with coal from the cellar. I was not a brave child, and to me the corners of the cellar seemed menacing and full of queer, moving shadows—wolves? robbers? I cannot remember when I first started taking the thought of Nathan Hale down cellar with me, for a shield and buckler. I thought, "If he could be hanged, I can go down cellar."

The thing was, he was no impossible hero; he was a member of the family; and he was young, too. He was a hero you could take along with you into the cellar of a New England farmhouse. You felt he'd be likely to say, "Aren't any wolves or robbers back there that I can see."

Well, I am grown up now and I know very little more about Nathan Hale than I did then. There are, of course, a mass of details about his short life. A devoted scholar named Seymour has spent years in collecting material about him. There's a wartime diary. He played football and checkers at camp. He drank wine at Brown's Tavern and cider at Stone's. But when you add all these little things you only affirm the peculiar simplicity of the story.

Hale is a symbol of all the young American men who fight and who die for us. He is a symbol partly because he was the first of our own heroes in the first of our own wars. He was among the first to show the world what Americans are made of. The reason the British destroyed his last letters home at the time of his death was, they said, so that "the rebels should not know they have a man who can die so firmly." He showed them.

He is no Washington or Jefferson although he ranks with the heroes. Washington was a great general and Jefferson was a genius. All of our nation's heroes are great men who are great by their minds and by their deeds and by their careers. All except Hale. His special gift to his country, and to us who love that country, was the manner of his death.

He is the young American. He is the patron of all the young Americans who have grown up, as he did, in quiet self-respecting families; who have gone to college and done well, and had fun, too; who have started out along their life's careers, well spoken of, promising; and then broken off to join their country's forces in time of war without an instant's hesitation; knowing what must be done and who must do it. He was no different from them. He was an American boy.

Everything that can be said of them can be said of him. In the letters of his friends written about him after his death, certain words keep cropping up. They sound oddly familiar. "Promising . . . patriotic . . . generous . . . modest . . . high-spirited . . . devoted. . . ." His friends fitted the words to Hale. They fit Americans.

Nothing was more American than Hale than his taking on the duties that led to his death. It was a dirty job, spying. Nobody wanted it. He took it. There's something about that, taking on a dirty job that's got to be done, that rings a bell. It's an American custom of American heroes.

Hale wasn't a remarkably articulate boy. His letters are nothing special. He just jotted things in his diary. But he became the spokesman for all young American fighting men who are willing to die for their country. He chanced to say the thing they think; the thing they mean, when there's not even a split second to think.

He stood there at Turtle Bay on Manhattan Island. Don't think he declaimed. He wasn't that kind. He had those few moments, and he was thinking about all the different things that were ending for him. He said, and I think it was more like a remark,

"I only regret. . . ."

("A Giant of the Revolution" was originally published under the title "Giant of Revolution Who Regretted He Had But One Life to Give" by the Richmond Times-Dispatch.)

☆ ☆ ☆

CONCERNING NATHAN HALE

I can now in imagination see his person & hear his voice—his person I should say was a little above the common stature in height, his shoulders of a moderate breadth, his limbs strait & very plump: regular features—very fair skin—blue eyes—flaxen or very light hair which was always kept short—his eyebrows a shade darker than his hair & his voice rather sharp or piercing—his bodily agility was remarkable. I have seen him follow a football & kick it over the tops of the trees in the Bowery at New York, (an exercise which he was fond of)—his mental powers seemed to be above the common sort—his mind of a sedate and sober cast, & he was undoubtedly Pious; for it was remark'd that when any of the soldiers of his company were sick he always visited them & usually Prayed for & with them in their sickness.

ELISHA BOSTWICK

NATHAN HALE

One hero dies,—a thousand new ones rise,
As flowers are sown where perfect blossoms
fall,—
Then quite unknown,—the name of Hale
now cries
Where duty sounds her silent call;
With head erect he moves, and stately pace,
To meet an awful doom,—no ribald jest
Brings scorn or hate to that exalted face,
His thoughts are far away, poised and at
rest;
Now on the scaffold see him turn and bid
Farewell to home and all his heart holds
dear,
Majestic presence,—all men's weakness hid,
And all his strength in that one hour made
clear,—
"I have one last regret,—that is to give
But one poor life, that my own land may
live!"

WILLIAM ORDWAY PARTRIDGE

If a soldier dies merely through the hazards of war, that is one thing. But if he dies for a cause to which his country has linked its destiny, such as human freedom or the maintenance of justice, he has linked himself to a cause which is great and glorious.

If that cause is eternal, an eternal significance is given to his dying. But if not, his attachment to it gives him the distinction of a patriot and a hero, but not necessarily that of a saint.

To die for justice, for freedom, links a man to something different from mere devotion to a flag. Justice is not temporal, it is eternal. In dying for it, one gives significance to his final act.

JOHN GARDNER

George Washington

Painting by James Peale in Independence Hall, Philadelphia

First in war, first in peace, and first in the hearts of his countrymen, he was second to none in the humble and enduring scenes of private life. Pious, just, humane, temperate, and sincere—uniform, dignified, and commanding—his example was as edifying to all around him as were the effects of that example lasting. HENRY LEE

The Character of Washington

By Thomas Jefferson

I think I knew General Washington intimately and thoroughly, and were I called on to delineate his character, it should be in terms like these:—

His mind was great and powerful, without being of the very first order, his penetration strong, though not so acute as that of a Newton, Bacon, or Locke; and as far as he saw, no judgment was ever sounder. It was slow in operation, being little aided by invention or imagination, but sure in conclusion. Hence the common remark of his officers, of the advantage he derived from councils of war, where, hearing all suggestions, he selected whatever was best; and certainly no general ever planned his battles more judiciously. But if deranged during the course of the action, if any member of his plan was dislocated by sudden circumstances, he was slow in readjustment. The consequence was, that he often failed in the field, and rarely against an enemy in station, as at Boston and New York. He was incapable of fear, meeting personal dangers with the calmest unconcern. Perhaps the strongest feature in his character was prudence; never acting until every circumstance, every consideration, was maturely weighed; refraining if he saw a doubt, but, when once decided, going through with his purpose, whatever obstacles opposed. His integrity was most pure, his justice the most inflexible I have ever known, no motives of interest or consanguinity, of friendship or hatred, being able to bias his decision. He was, indeed, in every sense of the words, a wise, a good, and a great man. His temper was naturally irritable and high-toned; but reflection and resolution had obtained a firm and habitual ascendency over it. If ever, however, it broke its bounds, he was most tremendous in his wrath. In his expenses he was honorable, but exact; liberal in contribution to whatever promised utility, but frowning and unyielding on all visionary projects and all unworthy calls on his charity. His heart was not warm in its affections; but he exactly calculated every man's value, and gave him a solid esteem proportioned to it. His person, you know, was fine, his stature exactly what one could wish, his deportment easy, erect, and noble; the best horseman of his age, and the most graceful figure that could be seen on horseback. Although in the circle of his friends, where he might be unreserved with safety, he took a free share in conversation, his colloquial talents were not above mediocrity, possessing neither copiousness of ideas nor fluency of words. In public, when called on for a sudden opinion, he was unready, short, and embarrassed. Yet he wrote readily, rather diffusely, in an easy and correct style. This he had acquired by conversation with the world, for his education was merely reading, writing, and common arithmetic, to which he added surveying at a later day. His time was employed in action chiefly, reading little, and that only in agriculture and English history. His correspondence became necessarily extensive, and, with journalizing his agricultural proceedings, occupied most of his leisure hours within doors. On the whole, his character was, in its mass, perfect, in nothing bad, in few points indifferent; and it may truly be said that never did nature and fortune combine more perfectly to make a man great, and to place him in the same constellation with whatever worthies have merited from man an everlasting remembrance. For his was the singular destiny and merit, of leading the armies of his country successfully through an arduous war for the establishment of its independence; of conducting its councils through the birth of a government, new in its forms and principles, until it had settled down into a quiet and orderly train; and of scrupulously obeying the laws through the whole of his career, civil and military, of which the history of the world furnishes no other example.

LETTER TO BENJAMIN FRANKLIN

If to be venerated for benevolence, if to be admired for talents, if to be esteemed for patriotism, if to be beloved for philanthropy, can gratify the human mind, you must have the pleasing consolation to know that you have not lived in vain. And I flatter myself that it will not be ranked among the least grateful occurrences of your life to be assured that, so long as I retain my memory, you will be thought on with respect, veneration, and affection by your sincere friend.

GEORGE WASHINGTON

Reason and experience both forbid us to expect that national morality can prevail in exclusion of religious principles.

GEORGE WASHINGTON

The preservation of the sacred fire of liberty and the destiny of the republican model of government are justly considered, perhaps as deeply, as finally, staked on the experiment intrusted to the hands of the American people.

GEORGE WASHINGTON
FIRST INAUGURAL ADDRESS

EXAMPLES OF DEVOTION

George Washington was one of the richest men in America at the time of the Revolution. His fields were well tilled and fenced. His mansion was beautiful and commodious. Prudence would have kept him out of the war and saved his property, but the love of liberty impelled him to stake his life and fortune on the outcome. When he won, we all won.

Moses could have lived in the King's court in safety, and perhaps succeeded to the Egyptian throne. He preferred hardship with his own people to luxury with the loss of honor and self-respect. And in his daring, the whole world profited.

The Pilgrim Fathers could have made a good living in England, or in Holland, but their dream of independence drove them to America and hardships. In their adventure and prowess was laid the foundation of idealism for the world's greatest nation.

The world owes some of its richest blessings and finest privileges to men who sacrificed the bird they held in their hand for better birds in the bush. It is an old fallacy that the certain is preferable to the possible.

SIMON EDELSTEIN

To lead a people in revolution wisely and successfully, without ambition and without crime, demands indeed lofty genius and unbending virtue. But to build their State amid the angry conflict of passion and prejudice, to peacefully inaugurate a complete and satisfactory government—this is the very greatest service that a man can render to mankind. But this also is the glory of Washington.

With the sure sagacity of a leader of men, he selected at once for the three highest stations the three chief Americans. Hamilton was the head, Jefferson was the heart, and John Jay the conscience of his administration. Washington's just and serene ascendency was the lambent flame in which these beneficent powers were fused; and nothing else than that ascendency could have ridden the whirlwind and directed the storm that burst around him. Party spirit blazed into fury. John Jay was hung in effigy; Hamilton was stoned; insurrection raised its head in the West; Washington himself was denounced. But the great soul was undismayed. Without a beacon, without a chart, but with unwavering eye and steady hand, he guided his country safe through darkness and through storm. He held his steadfast way, like the sun across the firmament, giving life and health and strength to the new nation; and upon a searching survey of his administration, there is no great act which his country would annul; no word spoken, no line written, no deed done by him, which justice would reverse or wisdom deplore.

—George William Curtis

WASHINGTON

Thank God! the people's choice was just,
The one man equal to his trust.
Wise beyond lore, and without weakness
good,
Calm in the strength of flawless rectitude.

JOHN GREENLEAF WHITTIER

This country and this people seem to have been made for each other.

JOHN JAY

LETTER TO MARTHA

It has been determined in Congress, that the whole army raised for the defence of the American cause shall be put under my care, and that it is necessary for me to proceed immediately to Boston to take upon me the command of it.

You may believe me, my dear Patsy, when I assure you in the most solemn manner that, so far from seeking this appointment, I have used every endeavor in my power to avoid it, not only from my unwillingness to part with you and the family, but from a consciousness of its being a trust too great for my capacity, and that I should enjoy more real happiness in one month with you at home than I have the most distant prospect of finding abroad. . . .

It was utterly out of my power to refuse this appointment, without exposing my character to such censure as would have reflected dishonor upon myself, and have given pain to my friends. . . .

I shall rely, therefore, confidently on that Providence which has heretofore preserved and been bountiful to me, not doubting but that I shall return safe to you in the fall.

GEORGE WASHINGTON

HISTORIANS' APPRAISAL

Washington was a giant in stature, a tireless and methodical worker, a firm ruler yet without the ambitions of a Caesar or a Cromwell, a soldier who faced hardships and death without flinching, a steadfast patriot, a hard-headed and practical director of affairs. Technicians have long disputed the skill of his strategy; some have ascribed the length of the war to his procrastination; others have found him wanting in energy and decision; but all have agreed that he did the one thing essential to victory—he kept some kind of army in the field in adversity as well as in prosperity and rallied about it the scattered and uncertain forces of a jealous and individualistic people.

CHARLES AND MARY BEARD

THE NAME OF WASHINGTON

America, the land beloved,
Today reveres the name of him
Whose character was free from guile,
Whose fame the ages cannot dim.

They called him proud, but erred therein;
No lord was he, though high of birth;
Though sprung from England's lofty peers,
He served the lowliest of earth.

He turned his back on pride of name,
On motherland and luxury,
To weld a horde of quarreling men
Into a nation proudly free.

Wherever liberty is found,
Wherever shines fair freedom's sun,
Men count America a friend
And bless the name of Washington.

ARTHUR GORDON FIELD

From WASHINGTON

Simple and brave, his faith awoke
Ploughmen to struggle with their fate;
Armies won battles when he spoke,
And out of CHAOS sprang the state.

ROBERT BRIDGES

From FIRST INAUGURAL

In tendering this homage to the great Author of every public and private good, I assure myself that it expresses your sentiments not less than my own; nor those of my fellow citizens at large, less than either. No people can be bound to acknowledge and adore the invisible Hand, which conducts the affairs of men, more than the people of the United States. Every step by which they have advanced to the character of an independent nation seems to have been distinguished by some token of Providential agency.

GEORGE WASHINGTON

THOMAS JEFFERSON, 1786

Engraved for Bancroft's *History of the United States* from the original portrait painted for John Adams by Mather Brown. (From the Emmet Collection, The New York Public Library)

Thomas Jefferson: A Day to Remember

CLARA INGRAM JUDSON

Thomas Jefferson shut himself up with his books for hours each day. He pondered on the works of Greek, Roman, French, and English philosophers, trying to select from their wisdom ideas that could be fitted to American conditions and needs. By July he had summed up his thinking in an essay he called "A Summary View of the Rights of British America."

"When we meet, we shall have to write instructions for our delegates to the Congress," he said to his wife. "I hope these thoughts will be helpful." He put two copies in his saddlebag and left for Williamsburg with Jupiter.

The weather was muggy and hot. Flies followed the chaise in clouds. Before they had gone half the journey, Jefferson was taken ill with dysentery.

"I shall have to turn back," he said to Jupiter. "Take my papers and deliver them in Williamsburg. One is for Patrick Henry, one for Peyton Randolph—"

"But—" Jupiter began to object.

"Say nothing. Do what I tell you!" Jefferson was so ill that his tone was sharp. Jupiter got the papers from the bag and helped turn the chaise around. Then, reluctantly, he went on.

Jefferson never knew quite how he got home. He was very ill. Luckily the horse was familiar with the road.

In Williamsburg, Jupiter faithfully delivered the documents to the two men. Patrick Henry glanced at his copy and then mislaid it; he was careless about anything that must be read. Peyton Randolph began to read his copy. A startled look came into his eyes; he folded the paper carefully and said to a friend, "Come to my room this evening. I am asking some others, also. I have something from Tom Jefferson that needs thought."

That evening behind a closed door, Randolph spread out Jefferson's paper and explained how it came to him.

"The paper is wise and thoughtful, but very bold. Tom reviews the settlement of America and reminds us that individual men, not the English government, opened up the new world. They fought for themselves; they lived under laws accepted in England. They must continue as free men."

Randolph glanced up. Men were listening intently.

"Tom points out definite injustices; we all resent it that a man cannot even make a hat from a coonskin he hunted on his own land. We must send our own iron overseas for manufacture. We make shippers rich and ourselves poor. The Stamp Act, the closing of the Port of Boston, taking away the right of trial by jury —but let me read you what he says:

" 'If the pulse of his[1] people shall beat calmly under

[1]his: the king's.

this experiment, another and another will be tried, until the measure of despotism be filled up.' You gentlemen must read the paper; I find it bold, perhaps too daring. Tom does not smooth over anything; 'Let those flatter who fear: it is not an American art,' he writes; 'the whole art of government consists in the art of being honest. The God who gave us life, gave us liberty at the same time.' He ends with a prayer for harmony. You should read this yourselves."

A murmur of shock, even fear, was heard. Men eyed each other uneasily. Later several agreed that the paper was interesting but much too bold. In the end, instructions of great mildness were voted for the delegates to the Continental Congress.

Word of this voting came to Jefferson, convalescing on his mountain, and he was hardly surprised.

"I proposed too long a leap for our citizens," he told his wife, Martha, quietly. "Less revolutionary ideas are familiar; the leaders should not be too far ahead."

But the writing of that "Summary View" was not wasted labor. Randolph had it printed; George Washington and many other Virginians read it. Later it was issued in England and made a great stir. Its author was called an "outlaw."

Thomas Jefferson was now thirty-one years old and a successful lawyer. A year earlier he had declined to accept Mr. Nicolas' practice when that gentleman wished to retire. Now he decided to withdraw from his own profitable practice and give all his time and thought to government. He was already favorably known as lawyer, architect, botanist, musician, farmer, and somewhat of an inventor. Human beings now became his main interest—men and their relations with each other. From the time his "Summary View" was published, he came to be recognized also as a writer and a statesman.

The First Continental Congress opened in Philadelphia in September 1774. Thomas Jefferson was not a delegate; his suggestions for the delegates had not been adopted. But many men had read his "Summary View"; its bold spirit seemed to be present in men's minds.

When the Congress opened, Patrick Henry rose at once and made a plea for unity.

"The distinction between Virginians, Pennsylvanians, New Yorkers, and New Englanders is no more. I am not a Virginian, but an American." That use of the word was new.

A feeling of optimism hung over the meeting. Independence was not discussed. Now that the colonists had joined together, king and Parliament would be reasonable, and all would be well. The Congress adjourned to meet in a year "if wrongs still continued." That seemed most unlikely.

Governor Dunmore did not call a Virginia assembly in the spring of 1775; so county delegates, elected the year before, met in Richmond in March. Friction with England had not ended, as men had hoped. Another session of the Continental Congress was needed: reports must be heard and delegates instructed. Most Virginians were annoyed but still loyal to their king.

As delegates gathered in St. John's Church, this loyalty began to irritate Patrick Henry. "Can't they see that the king waits for submission, then plans more affronts?" he cried.

But the convention began agreeably, and older men tried to keep the loyal tone. A routine resolution ended with a wish that the colony return "to those halcyon days when we lived a free and happy people."

This was too much for Henry! He jumped up and demanded that the colony be placed in a state of defense. Men stared.

"I move a committee be appointed to arm and train for defense!" he shouted. Older men rose and tried to be heard above the confused babel of talk.

"What tempts us to war?"

"We are not ready! Where are stores, generals, money?"

"We must be patient. England really needs us!"

Opposition always inspired Henry. Now he rose slowly, impressive in spite of shabby clothes and a slouch. His low voice hushed the tumult. Men turned to listen as he recited colonial wrongs and demanded, "When will you be ready to fight? next week? next year?"

Over their rapt attention his voice challenged them. "Peace! Peace! There is no peace! . . . Why stand we here idle? Is life so dear or peace so sweet as to be purchased at the price of chains and slavery? . . .

"I know not what course others may take; but as for me, give me liberty or give me death!"

In an awed silence Henry sank to his seat.

Then there was shouting and a roar of talk. His motion to put the colony in a state of defense was voted on. It passed—sixty-five to sixty; close, but it was seen that the young, vigorous men passed it.

Soon the committee to arm Virginia was appointed. Its roster included Henry, Jefferson, Washington, and Richard Henry Lee. The young men of Virginia were on the march.

Toward the end of the session in Richmond, the Virginia convention elected delegates to Congress. Peyton Randolph was continued as the leader; Washington and Henry were also re-elected. Jefferson's name was not on the list. On the last day, someone remembered the governor.

"Suppose Dunmore calls a meeting of the burgesses?"[1] That would oblige Randolph to stay in Williamsburg. Randolph was the speaker of the regular Virginia assembly as well as leader of the delegates to Congress. "We should have someone in his place."

So Thomas Jefferson was elected to the Continental Congress—as an alternate.

Meanwhile, Governor Dunmore actually was considering a call for an assembly. Williamsburg was deserted. But he wondered whether it was better to call back rebel Virginians or let them scatter to their homes. Suddenly he thought of the powder stored in the powder house near the Green. Virginians might blow up the town! He had it moved by night to warships on the nearby river.

Virginians were angry when news of this midnight theft got around. That powder belonged to the colony, not the king.

Patrick Henry gathered a company of the colonial militia and marched toward Williamsburg. They were a motley lot. Tomahawks and rifles were standard equipment, and hunting shirts were "official" uniforms. The men were nearing Williamsburg when peacemakers from the governor met them with a generous offer of cash for the powder.

Henry accepted the purchase. Chuckling at their easy success, the men agreed to return home.

But Dunmore did not trust them. He fortified the palace and waited until Patrick Henry was on his way to Philadelphia before he ventured to call the assembly. The burgesses were needed, Dunmore claimed, to reply to an important letter from the prime minister, Lord North.

Peyton Randolph turned back at the governor's call, and Jefferson made ready for the journey to Philadelphia. At the last minute he decided to go by way of Williamsburg.

Jefferson was welcomed at the assembly and promptly given the task of replying to Lord North. Then, with Richard, he set out on the tedious ten-day journey to Philadelphia. Arriving in the city, they got lodgings at the home of Benjamin Randolph, a cabinetmaker.

The author of "A Summary View" did not seem a stranger. Congressmen hastened to greet this tall, ruddy man of thirty-two. Someone noted that he was the next to the youngest in the Congress. Certainly he made an excellent first impression.

"That Jefferson is prompt, frank, explicit, and decisive," John Adams wrote of him. "He will be given work at once."

On the fifteenth of June this year, 1775, George Washington was elected commander in chief of colonial forces. He was to leave at once to join the army near Cambridge, Massachusetts. Congress decided to send with him a document explaining to the troops recent political happenings. Soldiers would fight better if they understood that Congress believed the time for action against British injustices had come.

Jefferson's first task in Congress was to help write this paper. The document the committee turned out was a compromise between bolder colonials and those who continued loyal to the king. The stirring words of the final paragraphs were written by Thomas Jefferson.

After Washington departed, Congress went at the tedious business of raising and equipping an army. Even the news about the battle of Bunker Hill did not really unite Congress; men's ideas differed about the size and cost of the army needed. But a compromise was worked out on this, too.

In August, when Congress recessed, Jefferson went home. The quiet of Monticello was a joy after the tumult of Congress and a big city. He worked on roads and helped to lay out an enlarged vegetable garden, with asparagus, artichokes, and several kinds of greens not commonly grown. A gardener Jefferson had brought from Italy planted a vineyard on the hillside. The orchard was increased with nectarines, apricots, and new apple and cherry trees. There was even time for music.

Jefferson was about to return to Congress when the new baby, little Jane, died. He felt he must not leave his wife immediately; his going would add heavy duties to her daily tasks. The Carr children needed him, too. The month of September was almost over when he finally got off to Philadelphia.

He found Congress still wrangling about army rules and expenses. He saw that they were sick of debate and of each other. For himself he was miserable as days went by and he had no word from Virginia. Was his wife ill? Had she gone to her sister's? Were they keeping bad news from him?

"The suspense is too terrible," he wrote. "If anything has happened, let me know." But no letters came.

In December he went home. Each colony had but one vote; Richard Henry Lee was now leader of the Virginia delegation, and the colony would not suffer by Jefferson's absence.

He found Mrs. Jefferson very frail and decided to stay until she improved. So it happened that during those winter months, while public opinion was changing fast, Thomas Jefferson was far away, on his mountaintop.

There he had time to read and to think. He studied a pamphlet called "Common Sense," written by an Englishman, Thomas Paine, who had come to America at the suggestion of Dr. Franklin. The paper was published early in 1776, and by late spring ten thousand copies had been sold.

[1] burgesses: representatives in the House of Burgesses, the legislative assembly of colonial Virginia.

Paine wrote: "Government even in its best state is but a necessary evil; in its worst, an intolerable one. . . . Ye that dare oppose not only tyranny, but the tyrant, stand forth!" Readers were stirred by such heady words. It was said that Washington called it "sound doctrine."

Trouble in Massachusetts[1] had been dramatic, and had her dangers, too. The British had set Norfolk on fire; a slave rebellion, thought to be inspired by the British, was attempted. Planters along the rivers were harassed. John Page feared his beautiful Rosewell might be burned.[2]

In Virginia, as in New England, the cautious mood of a few months earlier was changing to rebellion. Virginia delegates to the Third Continental Congress, meeting May 1776, were instructed to propose that the colonies be free and independent states and that the Congress appoint a committee to write a declaration of independence and a plan for a new government.

This same spring Jefferson was still living the quiet life of a country gentleman. He stocked his woods with deer and daily took the children out to feed them. Then he went to his office, a one-room building opposite his first bachelor quarters. There he studied and wrote letters by the hour.

Mrs. Jefferson rejoiced in each day that her husband was at home. She improved, and he had begun to think of leaving, when his mother died. In April he was taken ill with a migraine headache, the first of many that were to plague him. But in May the time came when he must go to Philadelphia.

In Philadelphia Jefferson rented rooms from a bricklayer named Graff. Bob unpacked while Jefferson did errands. He had brought with him a drawing for a small writing desk which he wanted his landlord of the year before to make.

"That'll be a neat little desk." Ben Randolph was pleased to be remembered with an order. "I shall make it right away, sir. You'll be wanting it." In a few days Ben brought the writing desk, and Bob put it on the table. It was a handsome thing, though small.

In Congress, Jefferson was put on a Canadian Affairs Committee and given other duties. But he took time to draft a constitution for Virginia.[1] He sent it south by George Wythe when Wythe left for Williamsburg.

On the seventh of June, Richard Henry Lee rose and presented to Congress a resolution which the Virginia assembly had passed and sent to Philadelphia by Lee. At first men hardly listened; then the room was hushed in startled astonishment. Lee was reading bold words:

"The united colonies are and ought to be free and independent states . . . absolved from all allegiance to the British Crown." This from Virginia was amazing boldness. Men rose, shouting to be heard. The room was in a tumult.

Jefferson listened both to Lee's words and to the shouting. Then he whispered to a colleague, "The middle colonies and South Carolina seem not quite ready yet."

"Better delay the vote rather than risk defeat, eh, Tom?"

Someone across the room had the same thought, and a motion was passed to delay action until July first.

The room quieted, and a delegate moved to appoint a committee to prepare a declaration of independence from England. This was not quite as strong as Lee's resolution. It passed; and John Adams of Massachusetts, Roger Sherman of Connecticut, Benjamin Franklin of Pennsylvania, Robert Livingston of New York, and Thomas Jefferson of Virginia, were appointed.

"A nice choice, geographically," someone remarked.

The four who were present came together to arrange a time and place for meeting.

"Dr. Franklin is not well; suppose we meet with him," one said. "We should get at the work at once." So it was agreed that the committee would go to Franklin's house on Bristol Street. They found the statesman sitting in a big chair with his gouty foot propped on a stool. Windows were open; fragrance from his garden drifted in as the men pulled chairs around their host.

"Five is too large a group for the actual work of writing," Franklin said, after they had talked for a time. "I suggest that one man prepare a draft and then we all go at it."

"That man should be Jefferson," John Adams said quickly.

"Indeed, no!" Jefferson said, flushing. "The matter needs more competence than I possess, sir."

"John is right." Franklin ignored Jefferson's protest. "Virginia has taken the lead; a Virginian should write the paper. The middle colonies are not yet ready."

"The work will go better if New England keeps out," Adams remarked. "What with the so-called Boston Tea Party, Bunker Hill, and the writings of Sam Adams, we have the name of being dangerous radicals."

Franklin laughed—then winced with gouty pain.

"You see a British enemy behind every paper, John!"

"But I am right, believe me," Adams insisted. "A Virginian is needed for this work. Jefferson has studied and thought more on the matter than any of us." The others approved his feeling. So Jefferson went to his rooms, opened his new writing desk, sharpened a pen, and laid out paper. Then he began to write. Little Mrs. Graff, sensing important work, tried to protect him from interruptions.

"Mr. Jefferson is busy this morning, sir. Could you leave a message for him?" she would say to callers.

Bob had packed books, but Jefferson did not read. The time for learning from history was ended. Now he must shape the best thinking of past philosophers into a new creed for Americans. Why now? Because the time had come when it was necessary to separate from old ties, when men of a new world should stand alone. He dipped a pen in the inkpot, and his driving thoughts sent it speeding across the paper.

"All men are created equal," he wrote, and paused. Were the people ready for that bold statement? Would they understand that the goal of political equality he stated was quite different from physical, mental, or economic equality no government could promise? Colonials had little education, on the average, but he trusted them to understand. One must have faith and make a beginning. He wrote on.

The document was days in growing. When Jefferson went out to eat, Mrs. Graff slipped in and tidied his room, cherishing every scrap of paper. When he did not leave, she brought him hot soup, nourishing meat, and well-cooked vegetables that he liked. He grew pale. He would not let Bob cut his hair; any fuss fretted him. He wanted only to think and to write.

The final words as he set them down were very simple: "And for the support of this declaration . . . we mutually pledge to each other our lives, our fortunes, and our sacred honor." There, it was written.

On Friday, the twenty-eighth of June, the declaration was read to the House and ordered put upon the table. On Monday, July first, the earlier Virginia resolution—that the colonies be declared free and independent states—was reopened, debated, and, on the following day, passed.

Then the Declaration of Independence prepared by the committee of five was taken up, and for two days members of Congress argued hotly over this phrase and that. Jefferson sat silent, flushed, and miserable. By July fourth, debate had grown acrimonious. The heat was frightful, and clouds of flies from the livery stable next door were maddening.

Late in the day the vote was taken; the Declaration was accepted. Jefferson sighed. Cherished sentences had been deleted; men were not ready for all he had hoped to include.

Jefferson left the turmoil of Congress, and as he walked on a quiet street, phrases from the paper drifted through his mind:

"When, in the course of human events, it becomes necessary for one people to dissolve the political bands which have connected them with another, and to assume among the powers of the earth, the separate and equal station to which the laws of nature and of nature's God entitle them, a decent respect to the opinions of mankind requires that they should declare the causes which impel them to the separation.

"We hold these truths to be self-evident: that all men are created equal, that they are endowed by their Creator with certain unalienable rights, that among these are life, liberty, and the pursuit of happiness. That to secure these rights, governments are instituted among men, deriving their just powers from the consent of the governed . . ."

Suddenly Jefferson was weary. "Perhaps the whole of it is overlong," he thought. "Perhaps those few words are the meat of it, and some day the king and his power, the colonies and their wrongs, will be forgotten. Today—or so it seems to me—we have taken a step on the road toward man's freedom. Perhaps July the fourth, 1776, will be a day to remember."

Summer night was falling. A welcome breeze stirred as he turned and went to his room.

[1] TROUBLE IN MASSACHUSETTS: the battles of Lexington and Concord had been fought in April 1775. The Americans laid siege to Boston, and on June 17, 1775, the Battle of Bunker Hill was fought.

[2] PAGE: a classmate of Jefferson at the College of William and Mary. ROSEWELL was the name of his mansion.

[1] constitution for Virginia: needed because Virginia had now declared her independence from Britain.

AMERICA has furnished to the world the character of Washington, and if our American institutions had done nothing else, that alone would have entitled them to the respect of mankind.
—Daniel Webster.

Can the liberties of a nation be thought secure, when we have removed their only firm basis, a conviction in the minds of the people that these liberties are the gift of God? That they are not to be violated but by his wrath? Indeed, I tremble for my country when I reflect that God is just; that his justice cannot sleep forever.

THOMAS JEFFERSON

THE MANY-SIDED JEFFERSON

Of Franklin's associates in the struggle for freedom and the founding of the nation, Thomas Jefferson was unquestionably the most distinguished. Gifted and versatile, this tall, gangling, red-headed young man from the Virginia frontier put his many talents to good use. He was a public servant in the very best sense of the term, as a member of the Continental Congress, as a representative in the Virginia House of Burgesses, as governor of Virginia, as minister to France, as first Secretary of State, as Vice-President, and as President of the United States.

His contributions to mankind were not only political. Jefferson planned a system of free public education for Virginia and founded the University of Virginia. A skilled architect, he designed beautiful buildings for that university. A scientist and inventor, he invented the moulded plow and the revolving chair. He was responsible for the decimal system of American coinage.

LETTER TO THOMAS JEFFERSON SMITH

Your affectionate and excellent father has requested that I would address to you something which might possibly have a favourable influence on the course of life you have to run, and I, too, as a namesake, feel an interest in that course.

Few words will be necessary, with good dispositions on your part.

Adore God. Reverence and cherish your parents. Love your neighbour as yourself, and your country more than yourself. Be just. Be true. Murmur not at the ways of Providence. So shall the life into which you have entered be the portal to one of eternal and ineffable bliss. And if to the dead it is permitted to care for the things of this world, every action of your life will be under my regard. Farewell.

THOMAS JEFFERSON

A NEW NATION

Some men look at Constitutions with sanctimonious reverence, and deem them, like the ark of the covenant, too sacred to be touched. They ascribe to the men of the preceding age a wisdom more than human, and suppose what they did to be beyond amendment. I knew that age well; I belonged to and labored with it. It deserved well of its country. It was very like the present, but without the experience of the present; and forty years of experience in Government is worth a century of book-reading; and this they would say themselves, were they to rise from the dead. I am certainly not an advocate for frequent and untried changes in laws and Constitutions. I think moderate imperfections had better be borne with; because, when once known, we accommodate ourselves to them, and find practical means of correcting their ill effects. But I know, also, that laws and institutions must go hand in hand with the progress of the human mind. As that becomes more developed, more enlightened, as new discoveries are made, new truths disclosed, and manners and opinions change with the change of circumstances, institutions must advance also and keep pace with the times.

THOMAS JEFFERSON

A nation which does not remember what it was yesterday, does not know what it is today, nor what it is trying to do. We are trying to do a futile thing if we do not know where we came from or what we have been about.

WOODROW WILSON

My God! how little do my countrymen know what precious blessings they are in possession of, and which no other people on earth enjoy!

THOMAS JEFFERSON

UNQUENCHABLE FAITH

On the Fourth of July, 1826, America celebrated its Jubilee—the Fiftieth Anniversary of Independence. John Adams, second President of the United States, died that day, aged ninety, while from Maine to Georgia bells rang and cannon boomed. And on that same day, Thomas Jefferson died before sunset in Virginia.

In their dying, in that swift, so aptly celebrated double departure, is something which shakes an American to the heart. It was not their great fame, their long lives or even the record of their work that made these two seem indestructible. It was their faith, their bounding, unquenchable faith in the future, their sure, immortal belief that mankind, if it so desired, could be free.

CATHERINE DRINKER BOWEN

JOHN ADAMS

Painting by Charles Willson Peale in Independence Hall, Philadelphia

The sacred rights of mankind are not to be rummaged from among old parchments or musty records. They are written, as with a sunbeam, in the whole volume of human nature, by the hand of the divinity itself, and can never be erased or obscured by mortal power.

ALEXANDER HAMILTON

LETTER TO HIS WIFE

The second day of July, 1776, will be the most memorable epoch in the history of America.

I am apt to believe that it will be celebrated by succeeding generations as the great anniversary festival. It ought to be commemorated as the day of deliverance, by solemn acts of devotion to God Almighty.

It ought to be solemnized with pomp and parade, with shows, games, sports, guns, bells, bonfires, and illuminations, from one end of this continent to the other, from this time forward forevermore.

JOHN ADAMS

In its main features the Declaration of Independence is a great spiritual document.

It is a declaration not of material but of spiritual conceptions.

Equality, liberty, popular sovereignty, the rights of man—these are the elements which we can see and touch.

They are ideals.

They have their source and their roots in the religious convictions.

Unless the faith of the American people in these religious convictions is to endure, the principles of our Declaration will perish.

CALVIN COOLIDGE

Liberty has been the key to our progress in the past and is the key to our progress in the future. If we can preserve liberty in all its essentials, there is no limit to the future of the American people.

ROBERT A. TAFT

Proclaim liberty throughout all the land unto all the inhabitants thereof.

INSCRIPTION ON THE LIBERTY BELL

THE DAY THE BELLS RANG JULY 4, 1776

During the day, the streets of Philadelphia were crowded with people anxious to learn the decision.

In the steeple of the old State House was a bell on which, by a happy coincidence, was inscribed, "Proclaim liberty throughout all the land unto all the inhabitants thereof."

In the morning, when Congress assembled, the bell-ringer went to his post, having placed his boy below to announce when the Declaration was adopted, that his bell might be the first to peal forth the glad tidings.

Long he waited, while the deliberations went on. Impatiently the old man shook his head and repeated, "They will never do it! They will never do it!"

Suddenly he heard his boy clapping his hands and shouting, "Ring! Ring!"

Grasping the iron tongue, he swung it to and fro, proclaiming the glad news of liberty to all the land.

The crowded streets caught up the sound. Every steeple re-echoed it.

All that night, by shouts, and illuminations, and booming of cannon, the people declared their joy.

From A BRIEF HISTORY OF THE UNITED STATES (1871)

LIBERTY BELL

One of the most cherished symbols of American independence is the famous Liberty Bell, now preserved in Independence Hall, Philadelphia. It has been rung on a number of occasions, the most important of which were the following:

On July 4, 1776, the bell was rung to announce the official adoption of the Declaration of Independence. This was actually the birthday of the nation, and marks the most important single event in its history.

October 14, 1781, it was rung to celebrate the surrender of Lord Cornwallis of the English forces, and the virtual close of the Revolutionary War.

April 6, 1783, it announced the proclamation of peace with Great Britain.

September 29, 1824, it was rung to welcome Lafayette, the famous French general who had assisted Washington, to Independence Hall.

July 4, 1826, it tolled to announce the death of Thomas Jefferson, principal author of the Declaration of Independence.

July 14, 1826, it ushered in "The Year of Jubilee," the fiftieth anniversary of the American Republic.

July 4, 1831, the famous bell rang for the last time on Independence Day.

February 22, 1832, the bell was rung to commemorate the birth of George Washington. Later in the same year it tolled to announce the death of the last surviving signer of the Declaration of Independence—Charles Carroll of Carrollton, Georgia.

July 21, 1834, it tolled again for the death of the Marquis de Lafayette.

July 8, 1835, while it was being tolled for the death of Chief Justice John Marshall, a crack developed in the bell. It started from the brim and inclined in a righthand direction toward the crown.

On February 22, 1843, when an attempt was being made to ring the bell on Washington's birthday, the fracture increased to such an extent that no effort has been made to ring it since that time.

RELIGIOUS TELESCOPE

That government is the strongest of which every man feels himself a part.

THOMAS JEFFERSON

It is refreshing to turn to the early incidents of our history, and learn wisdom from the acts of the great men who have gone to their account.

JOHN MCLEAN

RAISING THE FLAG ON IWO JIMA

A COMMITTEE OF CONGRESS VISITS BETSY ROSS

The committee asked her if she thought she could make a flag from a design, a rough drawing of which General Washington exhibited. She replied with diffidence and becoming modesty that "she did not know, but would try."

She noticed, however, that the stars, as drawn, had six points, and informed the committee that the correct star should have but five points. They answered that they understood this, but that a great number of stars would be required, and the more regular form with six points could be more easily made than one with five. She responded in a practical way, by deftly folding a scrap of paper, and then, with a single clip of her scissors, she displayed a true, symmetrical, five-pointed star.

After the design was partially redrawn on the table in her little back parlor, she was left to make her sample flag according to her own ideas of the arrangement of the stars, the proportions of the stripes, and the general form of the whole.

Some time after its completion, it was presented to Congress, and the committee soon thereafter had the pleasure of reporting to her that her flag was accepted as the national standard, and she was authorized to proceed at once to the manufacture of a large number for disposal by the Continental Congress.

GEORGE CANBY

BY ACT OF CONGRESS

(APRIL 4, 1818)

Section 1. Be it enacted, etc., that from and after the fourth of July next, the flag of the United States be thirteen horizontal stripes, alternate red and white; that the Union have twenty stars, white in a blue field.

Section 2. And be it further enacted, that on the admission of every new state into the Union, one star be added to the union of the flag; and that such addition shall take effect on the fourth of July next succeeding such admission.

BETSY ROSS FLAG

The Flag Goes By

Hats off!
Along the street there comes
A blare of bugles, a ruffle of drums,
A flash of color beneath the sky:
Hats off!
The flag is passing by!

Blue and crimson and white it shines,
Over the steel-tipped, ordered lines.
Hats off!
The colors before us fly;
But more than the flag is passing by.

Sea-fights and land-fights, grim and great,
Fought to make and to save the State:
Weary marches and sinking ships;
Cheers of victory on dying lips;

Days of plenty and years of peace;
March of a strong land's swift increase;
Equal justice, right and law,
Stately honor and reverend awe;

Sign of a nation, great and strong
To ward her people from foreign wrong:
Pride and glory and honor,—all
Live in the colors to stand or fall.

Hats off!
Along the street there comes
A blare of bugles, a ruffle of drums;
And loyal hearts are beating high:
Hats off!
The flag is passing by!

HENRY HOLCOMB BENNETT

From THE AMERICAN FLAG

Flag of the free heart's hope and home!
By angel hands to valor given;
Thy stars have lit the welkin dome,
And all thy hues were born in heaven.
Forever float that standard sheet!
Where breathes the foe but falls before us,
With Freedom's soil beneath our feet,
And Freedom's banner streaming o'er us!

JOSEPH RODMAN DRAKE

The Star-spangled banner

O! say, can ye see by the dawn's early light
What so proudly we hail'd by the twilight's last gleaming?
Whose bright stars & broad stripes, through the clouds of the fight,
O'er the ramparts we watch'd were so gallantly streaming?
And the rockets red glare — the bomb bursting in air
Gave proof through the night that our flag was still there
O! say does that star spangled banner yet wave
O'er the land of the free & the home of the brave?

On that shore, dimly seen through the mists of the deep,
Where the foe's haughty host in dread silence reposes,
What is that which the breeze, o'er the towering steep
As it fitfully blows, half-conceals, half discloses?
Now it catches the gleam of the morning's first beam,
In full glory reflected now shines on the stream.
'Tis the star-spangled banner — O! long may it wave
O'er the land of the free & the home of the brave

The British fleet next (September 12, 1814) moved on Fort McHenry, the chief defense of Baltimore. The fort held out valiantly against the furious bombardment; if it fell, the chief city of Maryland must fall with it. Among those who anxiously watched the attack was Francis S. Key, a young Baltimorean, detained as a temporary prisoner by the British. When the sun rose on the second morning he saw with delight that the fort held out and that "our flag was still there." The enemy had ceased firing and were preparing to withdraw. Taking an old letter from his pocket, Key hastily wrote on the back of it the first draught of the national song of the "Star-Spangled Banner"; the whole country was soon ringing with its patriotic strains.

THE STAR-SPANGLED BANNER

THE AMERICAN NATIONAL ANTHEM

Oh, say, can you see, by the dawn's early light,
What so proudly we hailed at the twilight's last gleaming?
Whose broad stripes and bright stars, thro' the perilous fight,
O'er the ramparts we watched, were so gallantly streaming.
And the rockets' red glare, the bombs bursting in air,
Gave proof through the night that our flag was still there.
Oh, say, does that star-spangled banner yet wave
O'er the land of the free and the home of the brave?

On the shore dimly seen, thro' the mists of the deep,
Where the foe's haughty host in dread silence reposes,
What is that which the breeze, o'er the towering steep,
As it fitfully blows, half conceals, half discloses?
Now it catches the gleam of the morning's first beam,
In full glory reflected, now shines on the stream;
'Tis the star-spangled banner; oh, long may it wave
O'er the land of the free and the home of the brave.

❖

Oh, thus be it ever when freemen shall stand,
Between their loved homes and the war's desolation;
Blest with vict'ry and peace, may the heav'n-rescued land
Praise the Power that has made and preserved us a nation.

Then conquer we must, when our cause it is just,
And this be our motto: "In God is our trust";
And the star-spangled banner in triumph shall wave
O'er the land of the free and the home of the brave.

Francis Scott Key

What So Proudly We Hailed

While most of us began a long week-end playing, sleeping or sitting in the sun . . . and some of us were hating, baiting and tearing America down . . . 40,000 people in Denmark gathered on a hillside to celebrate our Fourth of July.

Hundreds of thousands of other Danes watched the ceremonies on television. (A turn-out equivalent to 2 million Americans assembled in one place, and perhaps 20 million watching TV.)

The Danes have been doing this for 57 years. Because they venerate what so proudly we hailed: The pride. The principle. The unity.

When the Nazis went foraging for Danish Jews, other Danes hid them. All of them. When they took hostages and offered to swap them for Jews, the Minister of Defense announced, "There is no point in exchanging one Dane for another."

The occupation told King Christian to order all Jews to wear yellow arm-bands. He asked all *Danes* to wear yellow arm-bands.

"I shall be the first to wear one," he said, "And I consider it the highest order of Denmark."

No one in Denmark thought this was remarkable. All Danes simply, and successfully, defended all Danes. Isn't that what our Declaration of Independence was about?

Isn't that why Denmark honors our Fourth of July? And isn't *that* something to think about before the next long week-end?

—July 4, 1969

★★★★★★★

The nation's strength is in the people.
The nation's prosperity is in their prosperity.
The nation's glory is in the equality of her justice.
The nation's perpetuity is in the patriotism of all her people.

GROVER CLEVELAND

Love of Country

From "The Lay of the Last Minstrel," Canto VI

Breathes there the man, with soul so dead,
Who never to himself hath said,
This is my own, my native land!
Whose heart hath ne'er within him burn'd,
As home his footsteps he hath turn'd
From wandering on a foreign strand?
If such there breathe, go, mark him well;
For him no minstrel raptures swell;
High though his titles, proud his name,
Boundless his wealth as wish can claim,—
Despite those titles, power, and pelf,
The wretch, concentred all in self,
Living, shall forfeit fair renown,
And, doubly dying, shall go down
To the vile dust from whence he sprung,
Unwept, unhonor'd, and unsung

Sir Walter Scott.

The United States is the only country with a known birthday.

JAMES G. BLAINE

The flag is the embodiment, not of sentiment, but of history.

WOODROW WILSON

"A thoughtful mind . . .
sees not the flag alone,
but the nation itself . . .
the principles, the truths,
the history."

—Henry Ward Beecher

To develop fully your own character, you must know your country's character.

DWIGHT D. EISENHOWER

FIFTIETH ANNIVERSARY

Respected Sir: The kind invitation I received from you, on the part of the citizens of the city of Washington, to be present with them at their celebration of the Fiftieth Anniversary of American Independence, as one of the surviving signers of an instrument, pregnant with our own and the fate of the world, is most flattering to myself, and heightened by the honorable accompaniment proposed for the comfort of such a journey. It adds sensibly to the sufferings of sickness, to be deprived by it of a personal participation in the rejoicings of that day; but acquiescence is a duty under circumstances not placed among those we are permitted to control.

I should, indeed, with peculiar delight, have met and exchanged there congratulations, personally, with the small band, the remnant of that host of worthies who joined with us on that day, in the bold and doubtful election we were to make, for our country, between submission and the sword; and to have enjoyed with them the consolatory fact that our fellow citizens, after half a century of experience and prosperity, continue to approve the choice we made.

May it be to the world, what I believe it will be, (to some parts sooner, to others later, but finally to all,) the signal of arousing men to burst the chains, under which monkish ignorance and superstition had persuaded them to bind themselves, and to assume the blessings and security of self-government. The form which we have substituted restores the free right to the unbounded exercise of reason and freedom of opinion. All eyes are opened or opening to the rights of man. The general spread of the light of science has already laid open to every view the palpable truth, that the mass of mankind has not been born with saddles on their backs, nor a favored few, booted and spurred, ready to ride them legitimately, by the grace of God.

These are grounds of hope for others; for ourselves, let the annual return of this day forever refresh our recollections of these rights, and an undiminished devotion to them.

THOMAS JEFFERSON
JUNE 24, 1826

THE FOURTH OF JULY

Day of glory! Welcome Day!
Freedom's banners greet thy ray;
See! how cheerfully they play
With thy morning breeze,
On the rocks where pilgrims kneeled,
On the heights where squadrons wheeled,
When a tyrant's thunder pealed
O'er the trembling seas.

God of armies! did thy stars
On their courses smite his cars;
Blast his arm, and wrest his bars
From the heaving tide?
On our standards! lo! they burn.
And, when days like this return,
Sparkle o'er the soldier's urn
Who for freedom died.

God of peace! whose spirit fills
All the echoes of our hills,
All the murmur of our rills,
Now the storm is o'er,
O let freemen be our sons,
And let future Washingtons
Rise, to lead their valiant ones
Till there's war no more!

JOHN PIERPONT

Washington's Greatest Triumph

It was nine o'clock on the morning of October 17, 1781. Around the little Chesapeake port of Yorktown, the earth shook and the sky itself seemed about to crack open from the continuous crash of 100 cannon, pouring round after brutal round into and over the crumbling dirt parapets protecting what was left of a once proud British army.

Crouched in their siege trenches only 200 yards away, watching French and American soldiers wondered how much longer flesh and blood could endure such point-blank pounding. Allied gunners had knocked out every British cannon. Every house in town was a battered ruin. The harbor was full of burnt and sunken ships. Beyond, the masts of 36 vigilant French battleships blocked hope of escape by sea.

Suddenly atop the parapet in the center of the British works appeared a small red-coated figure, beating vigorously on a drum. "Had we not seen . . . the red coat when he first mounted," Lieutenant Ebenezer Denny of Pennsylvania said later, "he might have beat till doomsday. The constant firing was too much for the sound of a single drum." A moment later, a British officer waving a white handkerchief appeared and began walking toward the American lines, accompanied by the drummerboy.

There was suddenly, unbelievably, silence, as every gun ceased firing and the only sound that of the drummerboy beating away. "I thought I never heard a drum equal to it," Denny says. "It was the most delightful music to us all."

The officer carried an historic letter to General George Washington from Lord Cornwallis.

"Sir, I propose a cessation of hostilities for 24 hours and that two officers may be appointed by each side to meet at Mr. Moore's house to settle terms for the surrender of the posts at York and Gloucester."

Washington received the letter without any sign of emotion. But inwardly, he must have trembled. Here were the words he had waited six long, bitter years to see, at the last desperate moment.

Already, in Europe, France was moving toward a separate peace with England, in which American independence would have been just one of many items to be traded across the table by the world's two greatest powers. It was the French fleet that had trapped Cornwallis on the Chesapeake shore, French guns that supplied most of the shot and shell that had hammered Cornwallis to his knees, French money that had financed the American march to Yorktown. With this victory, American delegates could insist on independence.

But Cornwallis was not captured yet. In New York, the British fleet was putting to sea on that very day, with another British army under Sir Henry Clinton crammed aboard, to make a frantic attempt to relieve Cornwallis. The French Admiral, de Grasse, had already threatened to sail away to keep a date with the Spanish in the West Indies. There was no time to waste. Washington's crisp reply declared his "ardent desire to spare the further effusion of blood" but he gave Cornwallis exactly two hours to state what terms he hoped to get.

Cornwallis, ever hopeful of seeing the British fleet on the horizon, complained morosely but complied. The British were down to their last 100 mortar shells. Over 2,000 men were sick or wounded. The rest were all but completely demoralized by eight days and nights of relentless bombardment.

Cornwallis's answer was unsatisfactory and Washington decided to state his terms. He and his aides spent most of the night working on a letter. Meanwhile, he generously ordered the allied cannon to cease fire, and the men in the trenches enjoyed their first night of peaceful sleep in over a week. It was interrupted on the British side by a ghastly accident.

The artillery commander ordered his cannoneers to spend the night filling mortar and howitzer shells with powder, in case the shooting began again the next day. The artillerymen stole some brandy and got thoroughly drunk before they went to the powder magazine. Someone was careless with a candle. The magazine and 13 soldiers suddenly went skyward in an enormous explosion.

At dawn, a strange sound came drifting out of the British lines—the bagpipers of the Scottish 76th Regiment were saluting their conquerors. Not to be outdone, the band of the French Royal Deux-Ponts Regiment replied. Slowly then, the sun rose on an astonishing scene. From one end of the British lines to the other, the parapets were crowded with men and officers, and on the Allied side the ramparts were equally full. Both armies simply stared at each other, and the torn silent battlefield, as if they were seeing it all for the first time.

Washington's terms were delivered that morning. He told Cornwallis his men would be "marched to such parts of the country as can . . . provide for their subsistence." Once more he gave him two hours to accept—or a "renewal of hostilities" would take place. By noon Cornwallis accepted, and appointed two aides to meet with two of Washington's aides to work out in final form the "articles of capitulation."

The delegates met at the Moore House, a simple white frame cottage, still standing at Yorktown. They spent the day haggling over details that were very important to soldiers in the 18th century. The British wanted to march out with the "honors of war," which included the right to fly flags and salute the victors with some of their own music. Colonel John Laurens, the American negotiator, adamantly refused. Only a year before he had been part of the American army that surrendered to the British at the siege of Charlestown, South Carolina, and the British had refused them this privilege.

"But," said the British aide, "my Lord Cornwallis did not command at Charlestown."

"It is not the individual that is here considered," Laurens grimly replied, "it is the nation."

Washington got the final terms around midnight, and had them written out in three copies by morning. Under each article, he calmly wrote his approval or rejection—and sent them into the British lines for Cornwallis to sign first. He then rode to Redoubt Number Ten, a stone's throw from the British lines, where he was joined by the French commander, the Count de Rochambeau, and one of the French admirals, Count de Barras. Other ranking officers crowded around. Finally, the papers arrived. Washington signed without a word. So did the French. Washington told an aide to place above the signatures: *"Done in the trenches before Yorktown in Virginia, October 19, 1781."*

Now only the formal ceremony remained. For this, the British even issued new uniforms to anyone who needed them. Just beyond the trenches the allied armies formed two long lines, the French on one side in glittering white and gold, the Americans in worn buff and blue on the other side. Washington and his staff were at the end, facing Rochambeau and his staff.

About one o'clock, the British marched out, their colors cased, their bands playing a slow, mournful march. Necks craned to catch a glimpse of the famed Cornwallis riding at the head of the column. But the officer in magnificent full dress was not the fighting Earl but his chief of staff, General Charles O'Hara.

For the first few minutes, as the British went past, every man of them kept his eyes riveted on the French troops, as if trying to blot out those colonials on the other side of the road. Marquis de Lafayette, commanding the American light infantry, snapped an order, and a moment later the band exploded to "Yankee Doodle." As if on a string, every British head was jerked around by the sound and they stared, against their will, into the eyes of their ex-subjects.

O'Hara, maintaining the same attitude, tried to surrender to Rochambeau instead of Washington. But a French aide blocked him with his horse, the French general pointed across the road. When he explained that Cornwallis was "indisposed," Washington directed him to take orders from his second in command, General Benjamin Lincoln. He could play the protocol game, too.

Lincoln led the British to an open field, surrounded by French hussars. There, rank after rank, many in tears, they laid down their arms. One British colonel actually bit his sword in impotent anguish. Then came 28 British captains to surrender their regimental colors. The Americans had detailed 28 sergeants to receive them. The British captains strenuously refused to surrender them to anyone but an officer. Finally Colonel Alexander Hamilton arranged for the youngest officer in the American army, an 18-year-old ensign named Wilson, to receive the flags one by one and hand them to the sergeants.

It was all over by three o'clock. Washington had an aide draft a brief, totally undramatic victory report to the President of the Continental Congress. Another aide, Tench Tilghman, was given the honor of carrying it to Philadelphia. The story of his trip is the best possible illustration of the narrow margin between American victory and defeat.

When Tilghman arrived, he asked Congress for a draft of money to pay for the expenses of his trip. They could not do it. There was not one dollar in the national treasury. Finally, each Congressman contributed a dollar out of his own pocket.

—Thomas J. Fleming

Reprinted from *This Week* Magazine / July 4, 1965

Benjamin Franklin (1706-1790).

Benjamin Franklin Diplomat of the Revolution

Twenty years after his place in history was assured, Ben Franklin earned it all over again, starting when he was 70.

By Harvey Ardman

When the United States was born out of the Declaration of Independence in 1776. Benjamin Franklin was 70 years old. If he had died 20 years earlier, he would still be a famous man today. But he now had a dozen years as a formidable statesman ahead of him.

His achievements in his earlier years were sufficient to have made several men famous. Printer, publisher, bookseller, scientist, philosopher, fire "commissioner," community leader, tax and money expert, mail-service pioneer, military organizer, homespun journalist, linguist, educator, diplomat, propagandist extraordinary when it came to persuading people where their interests lay (and lover boy, too, for that matter), Franklin had it made in the history books well before he was 50.

Franklin is even interesting as a psychological specimen. His mastery of himself and his shrewd understanding of people have seldom been equalled, nor has his tolerant and humorous approach to manipulating others.

In 1731, he established the first circulating library in the new world. In 1743, he founded the American Philosophical Society, the colonies' first brain trust. He started an academy that grew to be the University of Pennsylvania. By the time he was 42 he retired from his printing business, having established his income with *Poor Richard's Almanack* and other successes. After that he devoted himself largely to science and became world famous in it in his own time. His kite experiment in Philadelphia, which proved that electricity and lightning were the same, led him to invent the lightning rod. He is the author of the + and — signs on your flashlight batteries, for it was Ben Franklin who identified the positive and negative nature of electric current. He also invented the Franklin stove, which threw off more heat and used less fuel than any comparable home heating device then known. He invented bi-focal eyeglasses.

His alert mind established truths that we now take for granted, sometimes from trivial evidence that had been lying around unnoticed all along. Nobody had ever established that general rainstorms and snowstorms are roughly circular "suction pumps" that usually move *into* the wind on their east and northeast sides (in the northern hemisphere). Franklin's sharp mind noted in mail from Boston that northeast storms hit there *after* they'd struck Philadelphia, though if the storm itself had come from the northeast it would have been the other way around.

Reprinted from *The American Legion Magazine* • May 1970

By the age of 70, the kindly, aging philosopher was ready to spend the rest of his life in contemplation and in correspondence with his many famous friends all over the world. But his own country needed him. It was about to begin a life of its own—and the best energies of its most talented citizens were urgently required.

Before the struggle for independence was over, Benjamin Franklin gave freely of himself and his many abilities. Many would say that he contributed more than any other man to the success of the young Republic.

The story of Dr. Franklin's contribution to American independence begins long before 1776, however.

In that year, the signing of the Declaration of Independence was the first united political act of the colonies. But the pressure for union—and independence—had been building up for years.

The first person to suggest such a union publicly? Benjamin Franklin.

The year was 1753. The French had just built a string of forts in the Western wilderness and the great Iroquois Indian confederacy, the so-called Six Nations, was now sandwiched between the British colonies and the French forts.

Until this time, the British had been the strongest power in the new world, and the Iroquois had made their peace with the colonies. But now the French were growing strong. The Iroquois began to wonder if they'd bet on the wrong horse. So they sought reassurances of British support if the French and the Indian allies of the French squeezed them.

The Six Nations first sent delegations to the Britishers governing the colonies. In Virginia, the Governor sent young George Washington to what is now Pittsburgh to get the French to pull back. He had no success.

At the same time, the friendly Indians had also petitioned Pennsylvania authorities, among them Benjamin Franklin.

To try to hold on to the loyalty of the Six Nations, the Governor of Virginia dispatched a few men to build an English fort at the forks of the Ohio, and he commissioned Washington to go with reinforcements as soon as the Virginia militia was ready.

At this time, the Governor of Pennsylvania sent word that militia from his colony might join the Virginians on the Potomac early in March 1754. These were separate British colonies at the time. Any cooperation was voluntary and not obligatory.

The Pennsylvania Assembly, meeting in February, wasn't so sure it ought to help Virginia. It reviewed its instructions from London—to defend the colony

CULVER PHOTOS

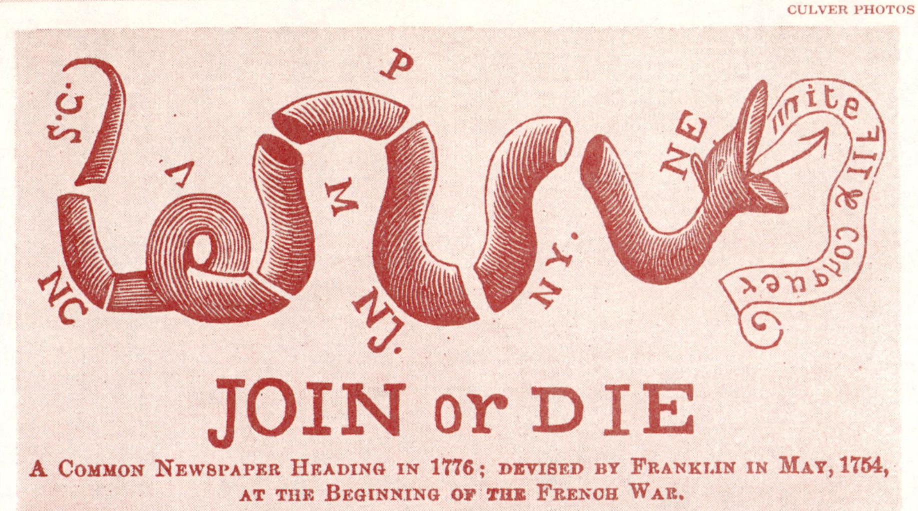

This editorial cartoon appeared in Franklin's Pennsylvania Gazette in 1754. It was a first call for Union of the 13 colonies, a step that would be taken 22 years later.

from invasion by the subjects of any foreign power, but to make use of armed force only within English territory. It was unclear whether the new French forts were within English territory or beyond it, the Assembly said. So the Pennsylvanians refused to appropriate money for the militia until the issue was clear.

In May, the small Virginia fort on the Ohio fell to the French and the Pennsylvania Assembly finally voted some money for defense. But they argued about how it should be raised and how it should be spent.

On May 9, 1754, Benjamin Franklin's *Pennsylvania Gazette* published what is now considered the first American cartoon, probably drawn by Franklin himself. It was a rough picture of a snake cut into eight pieces—labeled with the initials of New England, New York, New Jersey, Pennsylvania, Maryland, Virginia, North Carolina and South Carolina. The caption read "JOIN or DIE."

The problems with the French were the occasion for Franklin to begin publicizing his ideas for union—but not the reason. In fact, continental union was an idea he had been pondering for several years.

America, Franklin thought, should not be regulated from London. It was a dynamic country, spreading out across a continent, its population doubling every 20 years. England was static, in her ways. Americans, Franklin believed, should govern the colonies. They understood the temper of this land whose oldest families had been here 130 years.

In the early 1750's, Franklin really had no occasion to propose his ideas of union. True, England had levied laws restricting American trade and manufacture, and Franklin attacked the wisdom of these laws in print. But union? That was something else.

By the time the troubles with the French and the Indians began, Franklin had assumed an unusual position in the colonies. He had been appointed joint-deputy postmaster general of North America, a position of high prestige. More important, he was one of the few officials whose authority crossed colonial boundaries. On his long journeys of postal inspection, Franklin had come to know most of the influential citizens and had gained a firm understanding of the middle colonies and of New England.

Shortly after Franklin's snake cartoon was published, the Pennsylvania Assembly decided to send commissioners to Albany, to join the commissioners from other colonies in a new treaty with the Six Nations. Benjamin Franklin, of course, was one of those appointed.

The Albany conference had been called by the Board of Trade. It intended to cement the colonies' relationship with the Six Nations by giving presents and signing a new treaty. Since several colonies were concerned, New Hampshire, Massachusetts, New Jersey, Pennsylvania, Maryland and Virginia had been sent invitations. Virginia and New Jersey did not send commissioners, but Rhode Island and Connecticut did, without being asked.

On the way to Albany, Franklin discussed union with James Alexander, a member of the New York delegation and of Franklin's American Philosophical Society. He also wrote his ideas down and titled them "Short Hints Towards a Scheme for Uniting the Northern Colonies."

Franklin's union would still be British. It was to be planned by the commissioners at Albany, as representatives of their colonies, and established by Act of Parliament. It would be headed by a President-General, a military man appointed and paid by the Crown. A "Grand Council" would be chosen by the assemblies of the various colonies to act as the legislative branch.

This National Government—of sorts—would deal with the Indians, protect settlers against the French and perhaps equip ships to patrol coastal waters.

At the assembly, the commissioners debated Franklin's plan for union and adopted it. They then ordered it to be transmitted to the various assemblies, not only to those colonies that were represented, but also to New Jersey, Virginia and the Carolinas.

None of the assemblies approved Franklin's plan.

There were several reasons. One was the conviction that London would never go along with it. "Too democratic," one commissioner thought. "Gives the colonies too much prerogative," said another.

But the main reason Franklin's plan for union never came to pass was that the colonies were fiercely jealous of each other. None was willing to yield even the slightest power.

Long afterward, Franklin wrote, "The colonies, so united, would have been sufficiently strong to have defended themselves [from the French and Indians]; there would have been no need of troops from England, of course [to fight the French and Indians]; the subsequent pretence for taxing America [to pay for the French and Indian War]; and the bloody contest it occasioned [The American Revolution] would have been avoided. . . ."

Benjamin Franklin did not achieve a union of the colonies in 1754, but he planted a seed that was to flower magnificently 22 years later.

In 1755, the French and Indian War was on in earnest, with each colony acting (or not acting) in its own defense. British troops in ever larger numbers were coming over to wage the only resistance that was coordinated to any degree. Having failed to get concerted action, it now fell on Franklin and George Croghan to stir Pennsylvania to protect herself. Enemy raids on the western settlements (usually one or two Frenchmen with numerous Indians on the warpath) were burning outlying farms and communities and massacring the inhabitants.

Between its Quaker tradition of pacifism and its remoteness from the danger, the more populated eastern part of the colony was so complaisant that it took all of Franklin's powers to get Pennsylvania to put a militia of 1,400 in the field in 1756. The previous year it was only Franklin's cajolery and persistence which had raised enough supplies and transportation in Pennsylvania for the British General Braddock to make it overland with his army to attack the French at present-day Pittsburgh. (That Braddock suffered a terrible defeat and lost his own life was none of Ben's doing.)

Franklin was 50 in 1756, and by the time the French and Indian War was settled in the Treaty of Paris (as part of the Seven Years War in Europe) he was 58 and the American Revolution was still a dozen years ahead.

During those 12 years Franklin struggled to resolve the quarrels that were leading toward the Revolution. He spent much of his time in Europe, practically serving as an Ambassador at Large for the American union that didn't exist yet. Massachusetts, New Jersey and Georgia officially made him their representative, too. If you remember your history well enough you recall that the Stamp Act of the 1760's was the first British law that incited the colonies to rebellious acts, and that Parliament, in a moment of brief wisdom, repealed it in 1766. It isn't so well known that Parliament was persuaded to repeal the Stamp Act after listening to canny old Ben Franklin's advice, given by him in the House of Commons in February 1766. No other American was as well respected in Europe as Franklin.

But fresh injury and fresh rebellion followed and nine years later it all led to war.

After the fighting began in 1775 at Lexington and Concord, the early American effort against the British was sporadic and disjointed.

Part of the reason was an imperfect understanding among the people of what independence and freedom might mean, of how the colonies—as a separate nation—might be able to take their place in the family of nations.

In their different ways, many Revolutionary leaders tried to make the issues clear to the people and arouse them to passionate action.

The greatest figure among these men was Thomas Paine, a maker of corset stays who'd recently come from England. His words galvanized a nation:

"O! Ye that love mankind! Ye that dare oppose not only the tyranny but the tyrant, stand forth! Every spot of the old world is overrun with oppression. Freedom hath been hunted round the Globe. Asia and Africa have long expelled her. Europe regards her like a stranger and England hath given her warning to depart. O! Receive the fugitive, and prepare in time an asylum for mankind."

These words, and others written by Thomas Paine, helped to unify a country by making clear the ideals for which it might fight.

"The sun never shined on a cause of greater worth. It is not the affair of a City, a Country, a Province or a Kingdom; but of a continent—at least one-eighth part of the habitable globe. 'Tis not the concern of a day, a year, or an age. . . . Now is the seedtime of Continental Union, faith and honor. . . ."

It was "Common Sense." And it was a clarion call to freedom.

Throughout the Revolution, Thomas Paine wrote such words. They were a poor substitute, perhaps, for ammunition, for proper uniforms, for food for the army. But these words played a major role in keeping up the spirit of the Revolution in its darkest days.

Just who was Thomas Paine? How had he come to be associated with the Revolution? How did he happen to be in America? How did he happen to write

English-born Thomas Paine also came to America on Franklin's recommendation. He fought for independence via his writings, and became chief propagandist for the new nation.

"Common Sense?"

The answers to these questions lie with none other than Benjamin Franklin.

A year before the first shot was fired, the aging philosopher (now 68) was in England visiting friends, again trying to use his influence to get the Crown to soften its position toward the colonies. While there was still a chance for peace, Franklin pursued it with all of his energies.

One day, he was visited by a man unknown to him. That was surprising in itself, since Franklin either knew personally or knew of nearly every man of importance in Great Britain. His visitor that day: Thomas Paine.

Paine was not well dressed, nor was he well groomed. In fact, Franklin's servant had almost turned him away. But, for Benjamin Franklin, clothes definitely did not make the man. He saw Paine.

The staymaker had come to Franklin to ask a favor. He wanted to go to America and he needed a letter of introduction, something that would help him get a job.

Franklin quizzed him about his abilities and interests. Paine talked about making stays for corsets, about cobbling, about selling ribbons. And he mentioned that, on occasion, he wrote.

Then the two men talked about England and America, the opportunities in each, the governments, the ways of life.

In the end, Franklin wrote to his son-in-law in Philadelphia:

". . . The bearer, Mr. Thomas Paine, is very well recommended to me as an ingenious worthy young man. He goes to Pennsylvania with a view of settling there. I request you to give him your best advice and countenance, as he is quite a stranger there. If you can put him in the way of obtaining employment . . . you will do well and much oblige your affectionate father. . . ."

And so Thomas Paine came to America. But his acquaintance with Benjamin Franklin was not over. The philosopher-scientist appeared in another act in Paine's life that was crucial for the formation of the new nation.

Nearing his 70th birthday, Benjamin Franklin returned to Philadelphia. Despite his age, he took his place in the Pennsylvania Assembly and was appointed to the Committee of Safety, to plan the defense of the province. He was also made a member—the oldest—of the Continental Congress.

Meanwhile, Paine's fortunes had improved. He was now the editor of the *Pennsylvania Magazine*—and an ardent Revolutionary. The ideas that were later to take shape in "Common Sense" were already firmly in his mind.

Franklin and Paine renewed their acquaintanceship—exactly how is not recorded. They talked of what had happened in America in Franklin's absence, and Paine told Franklin of his ideas.

Out of that conversation came the idea that Paine should write down his feelings and beliefs, publish them in a pamphlet and distribute them widely.

At first, Paine had trouble finding a publisher. Many thought his ideas were treasonable and that publishing them would be extremely risky. But Franklin applied pressure on the right parties and "Common Sense" was printed.

Then, Franklin himself took 50 copies and sent them where he thought they would do the most good. Soon, "Common Sense" had turned into a wild best seller in the colonies.

With this, Thomas Paine became the chief propagandist for the new nation, the man who could move others to action, putting into words what they only sensed.

Eventually, his words were to significantly influence the formation of American foreign policy, and to inspire other writings by John Adams and Thomas Jefferson.

Perhaps the Revolution would have succeeded without Thomas Paine and "Common Sense." There is no way of knowing. But this nation's debt to him is clear. And it is also a debt to Benjamin Franklin.

Despite the increasing unity of the American people, there were many moments when all seemed lost. After the Continental Army, commanded by George Washington, was routed from Brooklyn, chased out of New York City and pursued through New Jersey, things seemed black indeed for the American cause.

The army rallied, of course, and Washington's hit and run tactics in New Jersey added steel to every member of his ragtag band. But the winter that fol-

THE BETTMANN ARCHIVE

Prussia's Baron von Steuben. With American fortunes waning after Valley Forge, he arrived on the scene, thanks to Franklin, to shape our ragged forces into a real army.

lowed seemed destined to again reduce the morale of the American forces, this time perhaps fatally.

Yet that did not happen. Washington's men left Valley Forge, after a terrible and debilitating winter, transformed into a highly disciplined army, a fighting force that matched in sheer professionalism the best the British could come up with.

Why didn't the American Army simply fade away after Valley Forge, especially with enlistments running out and victory apparently further away than ever? What welded the army into a fighting force to be reckoned with?

George Washington's courage and leadership were major factors in holding the army together. But another man, a Prussian, one of the foremost professional soldiers in Europe, molded the haphazard forces into a fighting unit. That man was Baron Friedrich Wilhelm von Steuben.

Without Baron von Steuben, it is difficult to see how the Continental Army could have forged the victories it did. Without him, it is easy to imagine a courageous but still untrained army scattered to the winds by the superior tactics and discipline of British soldiers.

But, if it weren't for Benjamin Franklin, Baron von Steuben would never have lent his talents to the American cause, and General Washington would never have welcomed the Prussian.

With American fortunes apparently waning, the French, America's ally and Britain's enemy, were worried. They wanted to help the infant nation—they were already sending ammunition and cannon and everything else they could. But how could they make the Continental Army good enough to withstand the British challenge?

The Frenchmen in charge of aiding America's war effort knew that Washington was an able and resolute leader, but that he was not a highly trained soldier. What was needed, they felt, was a professional soldier of the first rank, a man who could whip the disjointed American forces into a real army.

BENJAMIN FRANKLIN

That man could not be French, unfortunately. It wasn't because there weren't many Frenchmen willing to go to America and fight. Many did. But the French Army was nothing to brag about.

There was an army in Europe that was. It was the Prussian Army of Frederick the Great.

At exactly this moment, the French officials aiding America had a visit from one Captain von Steuben. They knew him well and realized that his professional skills, gained while on the operational staff of Frederick the Great, were of the highest order. Captain von Steuben was *the* perfect man to help the Americans.

But despite Captain von Steuben's willingness, even eagerness, to serve the Continental Army, there were some very serious obstacles.

For one, the Americans had never heard of Captain von Steuben. Though he was an important member of Frederick's army, he was not in the kind of position that might bring the Baron faraway fame.

For another, Americans were getting tired of European dilettantes, amateurs with inflated military titles who demanded that George Washington be relieved of command and that they be placed in his stead.

In addition, von Steuben was only a captain. His prestige in Prussia did not reside in his rank. And, outside of Prussia, his rank did not carry much prestige.

The French wanted the Americans to accept von Steuben like a parent wants his children to take vitamins—for the same reasons and with the same problems.

It was at this point that Benjamin Franklin came into the picture. Franklin was now living in Paris, serving as the American Ambassador. It was his job to see that French aid kept coming, while he conducted a kind of diplomatic warfare against England. From time to time, Silas Deane was Franklin's co-ambassador.

The French brought von Steuben to Franklin's Paris residence to explain their problem and von Steuben's unique abilities. Together, the small group began to work out some potential solutions to their problem.

Very quickly, they realized that Captain von Steuben must be sold to the American Congress and people.

Then somebody had an idea. They knew von Steuben was only a captain, but no one in America knew anything about the man. In short order, the Prussian soldier became His Excellency, Lieutenant General von Steuben, complete with a military secretary, an aide-de-camp and a resplendent uniform.

Then, Franklin and Deane wrote letters of introduction for the distinguished officer. On September 4, 1777, they wrote jointly to General Washington:

"The Gentleman who will have the honor of waiting upon you with this Letter is Baron Steuben, Lieut. Genl. in the King of Prussia's Service. Whom he attended in all of his campaigns, being his Aide-de-Camp, quartermaster Genl., etc. . . . The knowledge and experience he has acquired by 20 years study and practice in the Prussian School may be of great use in our Armies. I cannot therefore but recommend him warmly to your Excellency, wishing that our Service may be made agreeable to him."

With the French providing the ship and the necessary funds, the Prussian officer set out for America.

For Franklin, that letter to Washington was full of white lies. He had exaggerated von Steuben's rank, his military duties, his closeness to Frederick the Great. But General Washington had no reason to disbelieve.

There remained a single problem. What if the Continental Congress asked to see von Steuben's Prussian certificates of service? That would expose the hoax for what it was.

Franklin and Deane cooked up a simple answer for that one. In a letter to Robert Morris, one of the most important men in Congress, Deane wrote that since von Steuben was not certain he would be welcomed by the Americans, he left behind his certificates of service, which he had with him on an earlier journey to Paris.

"I mention this," Deane wrote, "as he had proposed to send for them. But I advised him not to delay his setting out on that account . . . for I thought it would only be the loss of time." Deane's letter also mentioned that von Steuben had shown him and Franklin letters of recommendation from Prince Henry, Frederick's brother and a great general in his own right in many a campaign.

Von Steuben was assigned to Washington at Valley Forge when he arrived in America. And, in a few remarkable weeks, he made over the entire army. After that, it was thoroughly a match for the British. At Monmouth, the Redcoats were appalled to find the former colonial "rabble" fighting like professionals.

But without the calculated duplicity of Franklin and his group in Paris, the whole affair might never have occurred, or occurred in so favorable a manner. Again, Benjamin Franklin had been in the right place, at the right time, and had known exactly what to do.

While American Ambassador to France, Benjamin Franklin also wore the hats of American consul-general, director of naval affairs and judge of the admiralty. He not only worked with America's French allies on the diplomatic front, he also directed the united colonies' naval operations against England.

In this capacity, Franklin played a vital role in one of America's noblest battles, an action that brought fame to one of this country's most revered heroes, John Paul Jones.

Original wood engraving by Bernard Brussel-Smith

Jones was convinced that America was fighting its sea battles with England inside out and backwards. The Continental Congress had raised a small navy and built an almost pitiful fleet of ships. These ships attempted to break the blockade of the American coast —a blockade established by dozens of heavily armed English ships of the line.

Not surprisingly, they failed. In fact, the only American maritime successes worthy of note were by the small, pesky privateers. These ships harassed British merchantmen and forced some of His Majesty's warships to protect commercial vessels.

John Paul Jones thought the blockade could be broken entirely if the Americans could mount a real threat—even a small one—to the harbors and villages on the English coast.

The daring American got permission to go ahead with his idea and soon he and his ship were the subject of terrified discussions all over England.

Based in France, Jones talked frequently with Franklin. Jones kept trying to get a more powerful ship for his operations and finally did. He named it the *Bonhomme Richard* ("Good Man Richard," which is the way the French said "Poor Richard," after Franklin's almanac).

Together, he and Franklin cooked up a scheme that could have brought British forces racing home to protect the motherland. The idea was a joint land and sea attack on the English coast. Lafayette would lead the troops: Jones would command the ships.

Unfortunately, Lafayette was too occupied in America to set out on the venture. But Franklin and Jones decided to go ahead with the sea raids in English waters anyway.

In May of 1779, John Paul Jones set out toward the English coast with his flagship and two other vessels. He carried instructions from Benjamin Franklin.

In September, the *Bonhomme Richard* defeated a larger, more heavily-armed English ship of the line, the *Serapis,* in a monumental battle. It was the first major victory of the American navy. And it gave life to a faltering war effort.

The aging philosopher-scientist was not on board the *Bonhomme Richard* when it clashed with the British ship off Flamborough Head—on England's east coast. But again he had made his presence felt, and at a crucial moment.

Today, most Americans believe that the Revolution came to an end when Cornwallis surrendered at Yorktown, on October 19, 1781. And that did end the fighting. But it did not bring recognition and a peace treaty.

The true end of the Revolution came two years later, on September 3, 1783, when the English and the Americans signed a treaty at Paris. For those two years, while Washington kept his restless army intact at Newburgh and New Windsor, N.Y., against any resumption of the war, Benjamin Franklin was America's foremost warrior. It was his diplomacy, intellect and guile that won the peace.

Franklin had always been concerned with peace. "I never knew a good war nor a bad peace," he had said. But this concern—despite some Congressional worries—did not make him a soft touch for the British. Quite the contrary. He had a very good idea of what a bad peace might be, and prepared to prevent one.

Even before the victory over Cornwallis, the new American nation had begun to angle for peace. In February of 1780, John Adams visited Paris secretly to explore with the French the possibilities of peace.

Adams' visit to Paris turned out to be a disaster. An intellect and a patriot, Adams was evidently not much of a diplomat. He quickly managed to infuriate those in France most involved with giving aid to America.

Franklin, somewhat slighted when Congress sent Adams over, managed not only to placate the French, but also to get another large loan from them.

Meanwhile, he threatened to resign from his position. Congress promptly gave him what he really had wanted—a stirring vote of confidence.

With Cornwallis' defeat, the outlook for peace brightened, but negotiations became far more complex. Because of interlocking treaties, the War for Independence involved not just the United States and England, but also France, Spain and Holland. Our treaty with France provided that neither party would make a separate peace. And France had a similar treaty with Spain and with Holland.

In effect, America needed the agreement of these three foreign countries before it could conclude peace with England. And Spain, for one, wasn't even interested in American independence. It just wanted to get its hands on Gibraltar.

To compound the confusion, Congress appointed five peace commissioners: Franklin, John Adams, John Jay, Henry Laurens and Thomas Jefferson. But Adams was in Holland, Jay was in Spain, Laurens, captured at sea, was a prisoner in the Tower of London (later, Franklin arranged for his release, in exchange for Burgoyne) and Jefferson was in America. That left Franklin to handle negotiations.

The peace talks began as a result of Franklin's personal relationship with a Madame Brillon, a neighbor and a friend. She knew an important Englishman, Lord Cholmondeley (pronounced Chumley), and he, in turn, was well acquainted with Lord Shelburne, England's new secretary for colonial affairs and the man with whom the peace would have to be made.

Franklin also knew Shelburne, but, until the Cholmondeley link appeared, had no easy way to contact him from Paris. Soon, Franklin passed Shelburne a note via Cholmondeley. It congratulated Shelburne on his new position and expressed hopes for an eventual peace between the nations.

This was all that was necessary to get negotiations under way.

A Mr. Oswald brought Franklin a reply from Shelburne. Oswald told Franklin that the new ministry sincerely wished for peace and that American independence was probably not a bone of contention any more.

Franklin realized that this was a request for a peace proposal, so he set out to design one. It had to be a proposal that would guarantee American interests, but not one that might humiliate England and set the war off again. Franklin decided to ask for more than he expected to get, to be sure he got what he wanted.

By the time Oswald reported back to Lord Shelburne, he was completely under Franklin's spell. The aging philosopher had told Oswald that he thought it would be a good idea for England to cede Canada and Nova Scotia to the United States, as part of the reparations England owed for having been the aggressor in the war and for having used Indians in "scalping and burning parties." (A paper of Franklin's two decades earlier is usually thought to have persuaded England to take Canada from the French instead of Guadeloupe in the settlement of the Seven Years War.)

In making this new suggestion, Franklin knew he was playing on opposition attitudes in England. Use of the Indians had always been opposed by a significant minority there. Now, Franklin thought, that attitude might be used to win a better peace for America.

In presenting this idea to Oswald, Franklin gave him a note stating his reasons. Oswald said he agreed completely.

To back all of this up, Franklin pulled off one of his most famous hoaxes. It was a printed "Supplement to the Boston Independent Chronicle," actually written by Franklin and published in Paris.

The "supplement" mentioned the real editor's name, was properly numbered and contained the kind of ads frequently seen in the actual newspaper: "Strayed or stolen from the subscriber, living at Salem, a bay horse, about seven years old, a stocky well set horse, marked I.C. on his off thigh, trots all. Whoever shall take up said horse and return him to the owner shall be handsomely rewarded. Henry White."

But the news items packed an altogether different sort of punch. They talked about a shipment of colonists' scalps the Seneca Indians were readying for England: "43 scalps of Congress soldiers, 98 of farmers killed in their houses, 97 of farmers killed in their fields, 102 farmers killed in different places and different ways, 88 scalps of women, 193 of boys and 211 of girls, among them 29 labeled to show that they were ripped out of their mothers' bellies."

This was gruesome propaganda and it spread all over the European continent like lightning. But Franklin knew it might achieve his aim: to turn the public against the previous British ministry and to make the present one unable to deny American demands.

On July 8, 1782, having dealt with France and her allies, Franklin wrote down for Oswald the terms of the peace: complete independence, recognition of boundaries, freedom of fishing off Newfoundland and elsewhere. The demand to cede Canada—designed to insure the more important demands—was "advised," but not insisted upon.

After this, the English stalled a while. They met with other peace commissioners and wrangled for nearly a year, accomplishing little. As the moment drew near for signing, the English negotiators said they needed further authority from Parliament. But Franklin was fully prepared for this. He produced a paper from his pocket and said that if there was going to be further delay, the Americans would demand payment for the goods that Gage had seized in Boston and Howe in Philadelphia; for all the tobacco, rice, etc., taken by Cornwallis; for all the ships and cargoes captured by the British Navy, and for all the villages and farms burned or destroyed during the war.

The English negotiators consulted with each other for a few minutes, then they returned to the table where the treaty was laid out. With Franklin watching, they signed. Now the War for Independence was really over.

When it had begun, Franklin was an old man. When he returned to America after serving his country in France, he was a very old man—just four months short of his 80th birthday. Yet his service to the United States of America was not over by a long shot.

After a tumultuous welcome home, Franklin was thoroughly ready to relax, to devote what remained of his life to philosophy. But within 24 hours of his arrival, he was besieged by two rival groups. One wished to revise the Pennsylvania constitution, the other wanted to leave it alone. They wanted him to run for the state's Supreme Executive Council.

Franklin agreed and was finally nominated by all of the parties in the contest. Shortly afterward, he was elected to the presidency—the governorship—of Pennsylvania.

Less than a year later, Franklin was in the midst of a new controversy—whether or not the Articles of Confederation under which the colonies had first been joined were sufficient for a United States. Franklin was among those favoring a stronger central government.

In March 1787, Benjamin Franklin was added to the Pennsylvania delegation to the Constitutional Convention, and, on May 25, he took his seat when it assembled to draft our present Constitution.

His mind "as keen as any 25-year-old's," according to one observer, Benjamin Franklin and George Washington, who served as chairman of the convention, were the two irreplaceable symbols of nationhood, the two giants of the Revolution.

And there is evidence that they recognized each other's importance. When George Washington arrived in Philadelphia, the first thing he did after his baggage was unloaded was to travel down Market Street to visit the man commonly believed to be the wisest in the world.

Franklin and Washington, along with James Madison, James Wilson and the other leading political figures of that day knew the importance of this convention. If it succeeded, it would give America strength and guidance for centuries to come. If it failed, it could signal the beginning of distrust and dissolution. The old Articles of Confederation were just the barest recognition of Franklin's old slogan, "JOIN or DIE."

As the convention got under way, the major source of conflict between delegates soon became apparent. The small, sparsely populated states wanted to be thought the equals of the larger states, with equal representation in the legislature. The larger states, however, felt that their population entitled them to a greater say.

There was no progress in resolving this conflict on the floor of the convention, so it was decided to put the matter into the hands of a committee. There were representatives of both views on the committee, but, more important, there were compromisers and peacemakers. One of these was Benjamin Franklin.

From July 2 to July 16, the committee fought and bargained. On the 16th, it voted on Franklin's motion to accept the "Great Compromise," two houses of Congress, one based on population (the House), and the other on equal representation from each state (the Senate). During those two weeks, Franklin's influence, bringing reason and calm, made the difference. Some historians believe that without it, the whole convention might have failed.

About three weeks later, Franklin's still agile mind made itself felt once again. Charles Pinckney, a young delegate from South Carolina, proposed that officers of the government be limited to wealthy property owners. He asked the convention to consider a requirement of "not less than one hundred thousand dollars for the President" and "half that sum" for judges and legislators.

The 81-year-old Franklin met the 24-year-old Pinckney head-on. He addressed the convention passionately, telling them of his dislike of everything that tended to "debase the spirit of the common people."

In the end, Franklin won. Pinckney's motion was rejected by so general a "no" that no roll call was needed.

When the time came to adjourn, with the Constitution finished, not all the delegates were perfectly pleased. It was a document full of compromises—as it had to be, if it were to unite a diverse people.

On September 17, the convention reassembled for the last time. The moment had come for signing. The Constitution was read once more to the delegates.

Then, Benjamin Franklin rose to his feet, with a speech in hand. Unable to remain standing for long, he handed it to James Wilson to read, then to James Madison, who was acting as secretary of the convention, to copy.

The speech was designed to create a good atmosphere for signing and to begin the campaign to get the separate states to approve it. It was Franklin's last major public statement, and it was Franklin at his best.

"Mr. President. I confess that I do not entirely approve of this Constitution at present; but sir, I am not sure I shall never approve it; for having lived long, I have experienced many instances of being obliged, by better information or fuller consideration, to change opinions even on important subjects. . . .

"In these sentiments, sir, I agree to this Constitution, with all its faults—if they are such—because I think a general government necessary for us. . . .

"I doubt, too, whether any other convention we can obtain may be able to make a better Constitution; for, when you assemble a number of men, to have the advantage of their joint wisdom, you inevitably assemble with those men all their prejudices, their passions, their errors of opinion, their local interests and their selfish views. From such an assembly, can a perfect production be expected?

"It therefore astonishes me, sir, to find this system approaching so near to perfection as it does; and I think it will astonish our enemies who are waiting with confidence to hear that our consels are confounded like those of the builders of Babel, and that our states are on the point of separation.

"On the whole sir. I cannot help expressing a wish that every member of the convention who may still have objections to it would, with me on this occasion, doubt a little of his own infallibility, and, to make manifest our unanimity, put his name to this instrument."

While the last members were signing, Franklin looked toward the President's chair, on the back of which was painted a rising sun. He observed to a few members near him that painters had found it difficult to distinguish in their art a rising from a setting sun. "But now at length, I have the happiness to know that it is a rising and not a setting sun."

Thus ended Benjamin Franklin's services to his nation. Shortly before his death, George Washington wrote to him:

"If to be venerated for benevolence, if to be admired for talents, if to be esteemed for patriotism, if to be beloved for philanthropy, can gratify the human mind, you must have the pleasing consolation to know that you have not lived in vain. And I flatter myself that it will not be ranked among the least grateful occurrences of your life to be assured that, so long as I retain my memory, you will be remembered with respect, veneration and affection by your sincere friend, George Washington."

Franklin's health failed rapidly as he passed his 84th birthday (Jan. 17, 1790). He didn't recover from a fall downstairs, and died on April 17. Today's Encyclopaedia Britannica closes his career well in a few words: "Philadelphia gave him a magnificent funeral. The French assembly went into mourning for three days. The whole civilized world was moved by the disappearance of the old sage who had done so much good during his long life." Benjamin Franklin shares an unpretentious grave with his wife, Deborah, in the Christ Church burial grounds at 5th and Arch Streets, in Philadelphia.

THE END

BATTLE HYMN OF THE REPUBLIC

Mine eyes have seen the glory of the
coming of the Lord;
He is trampling out the vintage where the
grapes of wrath are stored;
He hath loosed the fateful lightning of
his terrible swift sword:
His truth is marching on.

I have seen him in the watch-fires of a
hundred circling camps;
They have builded him an altar in the
evening dews and damps;
I can read his righteous sentence by the
dim and flaring lamps;
His day is marching on.

I have read a fiery gospel, writ in
burnished rows of steel:
"As ye deal with my contemners, so with you
my grace shall deal;
Let the Hero, born of woman, crush the
serpent with his heel,
Since God is marching on."

He has sounded forth the trumpet that shall
never call retreat;
He is sifting out the hearts of men before
his judgment-seat;
Oh, be swift, my soul, to answer him!
be jubilant, my feet!
Our God is marching on.

In the beauty of the lilies Christ was
born across the sea,
With a glory in his bosom that transfigures
you and me:
As he died to make men holy, let us die to
make men free,
While God is marching on.

JULIA WARD HOWE

Yorktown and Peace

When the news of the surrender of Cornwallis reached London, Lord North, the English prime minister, threw up his arms as though a cannon ball had struck him, and cried out wildly, "O God, it is all over!" He was right, for although desultory fighting continued for a time, yet the fall of Yorktown really ended the war.

Both sides had long been weary of the struggle. The spring after Cornwallis surrendered, the House of Commons resolved to "consider as enemies to his majesty and the country" all who should urge the further prosecution of the war against the Americans.

Before the close of that year a provisional treaty of peace was made (1782). On the 19th of April, 1783, just eight years to a day after the battle of Lexington, Washington issued an order to the Continental army declaring the War of the Revolution at an end. The soldiers had received no pay for a great length of time and they were in sore need of money; but Congress, as Washington said, sent them home "without a farthing in their pockets."

In making the final treaty of peace the main points which we demanded were: (1) the full recognition of the independence of the thirteen states; (2) the recognition of the Mississippi River as our western boundary; (3) the recognition of our right to fish on the banks of Newfoundland. The English, on the other hand, wished (1) to limit our western boundary to the line of the Alleghenies; (2) to shut us out from any part of the cod fisheries; (3) they insisted on our making compensation to the Tories for their loss of property.

Our commissioners, Adams, Franklin, and Jay, refused to accept these conditions, but agreed that the last demand should be referred to the legislatures of the states, with a recommendation that they give it favorable consideration. The result was that when the final treaty was signed at Paris, September 3, 1783, it fully recognized all the chief points which we claimed.

We the People of the United States, in Order to form a more perfect Union, establish Justice, insure domestic Tranquility, provide for the common defence, promote the general Welfare, and secure the Blessings of Liberty to ourselves and our Posterity, do ordain and establish this Constitution for the United States of America.

Article I.

Article II.

Article III.

Article IV.

Article V.

Article VI.

Article VII.

The Word, "the," being interlined between the seventh and eighth Lines of the first Page, The Word "Thirty" being partly written on an Erazure in the fifteenth Line of the first Page. The Words "is tried" being interlined between the thirty second and thirty third Lines of the first Page and the Word "the" being interlined between the forty third and forty fourth Lines of the second Page.

Attest William Jackson Secretary

done in Convention by the Unanimous Consent of the States present the Seventeenth Day of September in the Year of our Lord one thousand seven hundred and Eighty seven and of the Independance of the United States of America the Twelfth In witness whereof We have hereunto subscribed our Names,

Go: Washington—Presidt. and deputy from Virginia

Delaware: Geo: Read, Gunning Bedford jun, John Dickinson, Richard Bassett, Jaco: Broom

Maryland: James McHenry, Dan of St Thos. Jenifer, Danl. Carroll

Virginia: John Blair—, James Madison Jr.

North Carolina: Wm. Blount, Richd. Dobbs Spaight., Hu Williamson

South Carolina: J. Rutledge, Charles Cotesworth Pinckney, Charles Pinckney, Pierce Butler.

Georgia: William Few, Abr Baldwin

New Hampshire: John Langdon, Nicholas Gilman

Massachusetts: Nathaniel Gorham, Rufus King

Connecticut: Wm. Saml. Johnson, Roger Sherman

New York: Alexander Hamilton

New Jersey: Wil: Livingston, David Brearley., Wm. Paterson., Jona: Dayton

Pensylvania: B Franklin, Thomas Mifflin, Robt Morris, Geo. Clymer, Thos. FitzSimons, Jared Ingersoll, James Wilson., Gouv Morris

THEN THEY PRAYED

The Declaration of Independence was signed July 4, 1776. Our Constitution was introduced in 1787. From 1776 to 1787 various forms of government were tried and rejected.

George Washington referred to the period of eleven years as one of chaos and confusion. Mob attacks had been made upon the courthouse in Massachusetts and the congressional body had been forced to move from Philadelphia to New Jersey.

The Nation was bankrupt and seemed headed for anarchy.

In the face of these trying conditions, fifty-five men came to Philadelphia and framed our Constitution. Some of them walked, others rode horseback, coming many miles. They were not paid nor did they expect glory. All they wanted was a country of their own, wherein they could live in peace and happiness, and worship God according to the dictates of their own conscience.

For many weeks the framers met day after day without agreeing on a single line. On the last morning of the fifth week, in the midst of a heated discussion, they were about to give up and adjourn when Benjamin Franklin arose and addressed George Washington in the chair, [and] spoke as follows:

"Mr. President, the small progress we have made after five weeks . . . is melancholy proof of the imperfection of human understanding. We . . . feel our own want of political wisdom, since we have been running all about in search of it. We have gone back to ancient history for models of government . . . and we have viewed modern states all around Europe, but find none of their constitutions suitable in our circumstance.

"I have lived a long time, and the longer I live the more convincing proof I see . . . that God governs in the affairs of men . . . We have been assured, sir, in the sacred writings, that 'Except the Lord build the house, they labor in vain that build it.'

"I firmly believe this and I also believe that without His concurring aid, we shall succeed in this political building no better than the buildings of Babel; we shall be divided . . . our projects will be confounded, and we ourselves shall become a reproach and byword to future ages . . . I therefore beg leave to move:

"That hereafter prayers, imploring the assistance of Heaven and its blessings on our deliberations, be held in this assembly every morning before we proceed to business . . ."

From that moment the assembly began to make progress in the framing and adoption of the Constitution.

The makers of the Constitution sought to protect Americans in their beliefs, their thoughts, their emotions, and their sensations.

They conferred, as against the Government, the right to be let alone—the most comprehensive of rights and the right most valued by civilized men.

LOUIS D. BRANDEIS

LETTER TO THE CONSTITUTIONAL CONVENTION

We kept steadily in our view that which appears to us the greatest interest of every true American, the consolidation of our Union, in which is involved our prosperity, felicity, safety, perhaps our national existence.

GEORGE WASHINGTON

The ethical and moral concepts of Christianity are found all the way through the Declaration of Independence. It was on July 4, 1776, that fifty men gathered in Independence Hall in Philadelphia to declare this nation free from Great Britain and they affixed their signatures and then the Liberty Bell rang out. It was the birthday of a small nation that was to become the mightiest and greatest nation the world has ever known. Down through the years God has mightily blessed America.

BILLY GRAHAM

Congress of the United States

begun and held at the City of New-York, on

Wednesday the Fourth of March, one thousand seven hundred and eighty nine

THE Conventions of a number of the States, having at the time of their adopting the Constitution, expressed a desire, in order to prevent misconstruction or abuse of its powers, that further declaratory and restrictive clauses should be added: And as extending the ground of public confidence in the Government, will best ensure the beneficent ends of its institution

RESOLVED by the Senate and House of Representatives of the United States of America, in Congress assembled, two thirds of both Houses concurring, that the following Articles be proposed to the Legislatures of the several States, as amendments to the Constitution of the United States, all, or any of which Articles, when ratified by three fourths of the said Legislatures, to be valid to all intents and purposes, as part of the said Constitution; viz.

ARTICLES in addition to, and Amendment of the Constitution of the United States of America, proposed by Congress, and ratified by the Legislatures of the several States, pursuant to the fifth Article of the original Constitution.

Article the first. ... After the first enumeration required by the first Article of the Constitution, there shall be one Representative for every thirty thousand, until the number shall amount to one hundred, after which, the proportion shall be so regulated by Congress, that there shall be not less than one hundred Representatives, nor less than one Representative for every forty thousand persons, until the number of Representatives shall amount to two hundred, after which the proportion shall be so regulated by Congress, that there shall not be less than two hundred Representatives, nor more than one Representative for every fifty thousand persons.

Article the second. ... No law, varying the compensation for the services of the Senators and Representatives, shall take effect, until an election of Representatives shall have intervened.

Article the third. ... Congress shall make no law respecting an establishment of religion, or prohibiting the free exercise thereof; or abridging the freedom of speech, or of the press; or the right of the people peaceably to assemble, and to petition the Government for a redress of grievances.

Article the fourth. ... A well regulated militia, being necessary to the security of a free State, the right of the people to keep and bear arms, shall not be infringed.

Article the fifth. ... No Soldier shall, in time of peace be quartered in any house, without the consent of the owner, nor in time of war, but in a manner to be prescribed by law.

Article the sixth. ... The right of the people to be secure in their persons, houses, papers, and effects, against unreasonable searches and seizures, shall not be violated, and no Warrants shall issue, but upon probable cause, supported by oath or affirmation, and particularly describing the place to be searched, and the persons or things to be seized.

Article the seventh. ... No person shall be held to answer for a capital, or otherwise infamous crime, unless on a presentment or indictment of a Grand Jury, except in cases arising in the land or naval forces, or in the Militia, when in actual service in time of War or public danger; nor shall any person be subject for the same offence to be twice put in jeopardy of life or limb; nor shall be compelled in any criminal case, to be a witness against himself, nor be deprived of life, liberty, or property, without due process of law; nor shall private property be taken for public use without just compensation.

Article the eighth. ... In all criminal prosecutions, the accused shall enjoy the right to a speedy and public trial, by an impartial jury of the State and district wherein the crime shall have been committed, which district shall have been previously ascertained by law, and to be informed of the nature and cause of the accusation; to be confronted with the witnesses against him; to have compulsory process for obtaining witnesses in his favor, and to have the assistance of counsel for his defence.

Article the ninth. ... In suits at common law, where the value in controversy shall exceed twenty dollars, the right of trial by jury shall be preserved, and no fact tried by a jury shall be otherwise re-examined in any Court of the United States, than according to the rules of the common law.

Article the tenth. ... Excessive bail shall not be required, nor excessive fines imposed, nor cruel and unusual punishments inflicted.

Article the eleventh. ... The enumeration in the Constitution, of certain rights, shall not be construed to deny or disparage others retained by the people.

Article the twelfth. ... The powers not delegated to the United States by the Constitution, nor prohibited by it to the States, are reserved to the States respectively, or to the people.

ATTEST,

Frederick Augustus Muhlenberg Speaker of the House of Representatives.

John Adams, Vice-President of the United States, and President of the Senate.

John Beckley, Clerk of the House of Representatives.

Sam. A. Otis Secretary of the Senate.

THE BILL OF RIGHTS

I. Congress shall make no law respecting an establishment of religion, or prohibiting the free exercise thereof; or abridging the freedom of speech, or of the press; or the right of the people peaceably to assemble, and to petition the Government for a redress of grievances.

II. A well-regulated Militia, being necessary to the security of a free State, the right of the people to keep and bear Arms, shall not be infringed.

III. No Soldier shall, in time of peace, be quartered in any house, without the consent of the Owner, nor in time of war, but in a manner to be prescribed by law.

IV. The right of the people to be secure in their persons, houses, papers, and effects, against unreasonable searches and seizures, shall not be violated, and no Warrants shall issue, but upon probable cause, supported by Oath or affirmation, and particularly describing the place to be searched, and the persons or things to be seized.

V. No person shall be held to answer for a capital, or otherwise infamous crime, unless on a presentment or indictment of a Grand Jury, except in cases arising in the land or naval forces, or in the Militia, when in actual service in time of War or public danger; nor shall any person be subject for the same offence to be twice put in jeopardy of life or limb; nor shall be compelled in any criminal case to be a witness against himself, nor be deprived of life, liberty, or property, without due process of law; nor shall private property be taken for public use, without just compensation.

VI. In all criminal prosecutions, the accused shall enjoy the right to a speedy and public trial, by an impartial jury of the State and district wherein the crime shall have been committed, which district shall have been previously ascertained by law, and to be informed of the nature and cause of the accusation; to be confronted with the witnesses against him; to have compulsory process for obtaining witnesses in his favor, and to have the Assistance of Counsel for his defence.

VII. In Suits at common law, where the value in controversy shall exceed twenty dollars, the right of trial by jury shall be preserved, and no fact tried by a jury, shall be otherwise re-examined in any Court of the United States, than according to the rules of the common law.

VIII. Excessive bail shall not be required, nor excessive fines imposed, nor cruel and unusual punishments inflicted.

IX. The enumeration in the Constitution, of certain rights, shall not be construed to deny or disparage others retained by the people.

X. The powers not delegated to the United States by the Constitution, nor prohibited by it to the States, are reserved to the States respectively, or to the people.

If the Ten Commandments provide a standard of conduct for a virtuous individual, then the Ten Amendments which make our Bill of Rights are the ten commandments for a virtuous government.

PIERSON M. HALL

The liberty enjoyed by the people of these States, of worshipping Almighty God agreeably to their consciences, is not only among the choicest of their blessings, but also of their rights.

GEORGE WASHINGTON

It does not require a lawyer to interpret the provisions of the Bill of Rights. They are as clear as the Ten Commandments.

HERBERT HOOVER

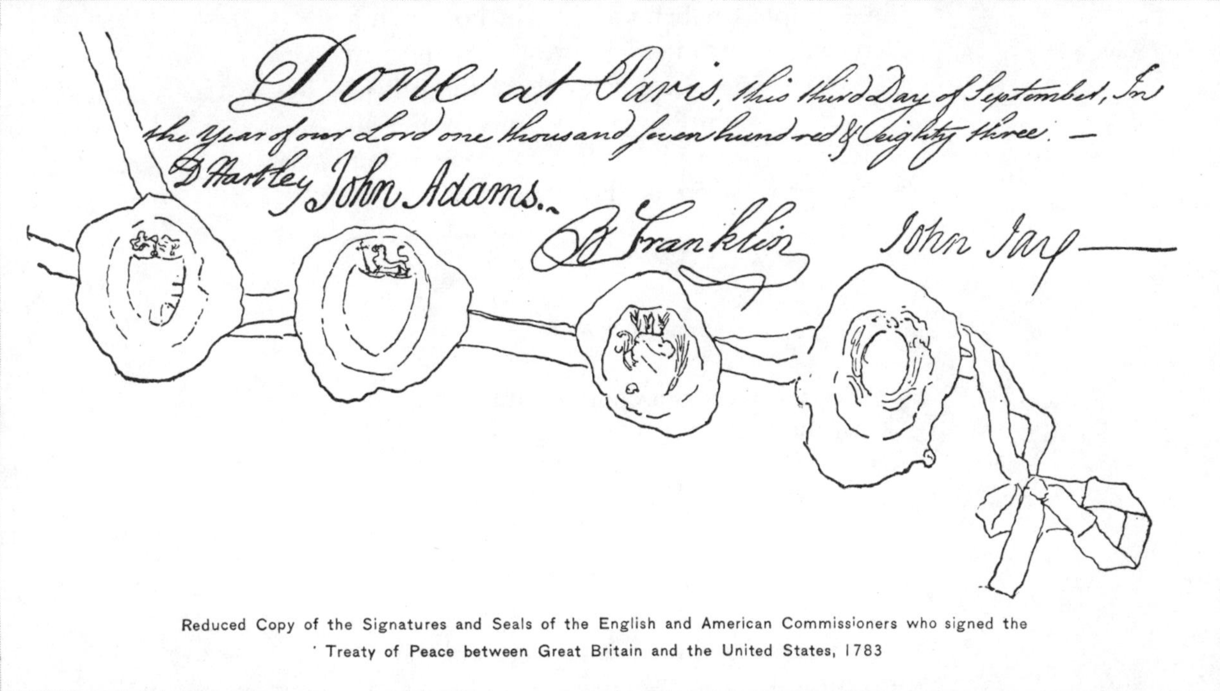

Reduced Copy of the Signatures and Seals of the English and American Commissioners who signed the Treaty of Peace between Great Britain and the United States, 1783

The Constitution of the United States is the result of the collected wisdom of our country.

THOMAS JEFFERSON

The principles of Jefferson are the definitions and axioms of free society.

ABRAHAM LINCOLN

Unlike the dashing Spanish adventurers, these simple English folk sought homes in a New World. Their interest was not in treasure — the "bright jewels of the mine" — but in beginning a new life, a life in which they would be free, among other things, to worship as they chose.

★★★★★★

Patriotism depends as much on mutual suffering as on mutual success. It is by that experience of all fortunes and all feelings that a great national character is created.

BENJAMIN DISRAELI

Man became free when he recognized that he was subject to law.

WILL DURANT

★★★★★★

FROM AN OLD ALMANAC

O! ye unborn inhabitants of America! Should this page escape its destin'd conflagration at the year's end, and these alphabetical letters remain legible, when your eyes behold the sun after he has rolled the seasons round for two or three centuries more, you will know that in Anno Domini 1758, we dream'd of your times.

NATHANIEL AMES

Growth of A Nation

A BILL OF DUTIES

We are, as individuals and as a nation, very justly proud of our Bill of Rights. It is, indeed, the cornerstone of our liberty. But once I heard a wise man say that in order to maintain and fulfill the Bill of Rights, we needed to develop a Bill of Duties.

Duty is an old-fashioned word—but all the modern sophistries will not wipe it out. This country grew up on copy book sayings, and it reached its heights under men who had had thoroughly dinned into them the plain homely virtues of loyalty, honesty and integrity, and who personally applied them to their community life.

We have wandered far from these copy book sayings, and have accepted our rights as special privileges for which no payment was necessary. We must go back to the Proverbs, to the simple statement of right and wrong.

> Righteousness exalteth a nation; but sin is a reproach to any people.
>
> He that justifieth the wicked and he that condemneth the just, even they both are an abomination to the Lord.
>
> Train up a child in the way he should go; and when he is old, he will not depart from it.
>
> Buy the truth and sell it not; get wisdom and instruction and understanding.
>
> He that hath no rule over his own spirit is like a city that is broken down and without walls.
>
> They that forsake the law, praise the wicked, but such as keep the law contend with them.

Only by setting up a Bill of Duties for ourselves can we observe the spirit as well as the letter of the Bill of Rights.

How well do you know this charter of our liberties? Read it over carefully and turn its clauses into inverse ratio. Free press—free to speak the truth but not free to make false statements. Free assembly—for free and friendly discussion, but not to be used to overthrow the government. Freedom to worship—but not to keep anyone else from worshipping. And so on. Each freedom that is given, carries with it its duty or restriction as it affects each man's conduct toward his neighbor.

If we will but adhere conscientiously to a Bill of Duties, we need have no fear of retaining the benefits of our Bill of Rights.

—Clinton T. Howell

AMERICA

My country, 'tis of thee,
Sweet land of liberty,
Of thee I sing;
Land where my fathers died,
Land of the pilgrims' pride.
From every mountain-side
Let Freedom ring.

My native country, thee,
Land of the noble free,—
Thy name I love;
I love thy rocks and rills
Thy woods and templed hills:
My heart with rapture thrills
Like that above.

Let music swell the breeze,
And ring from all the trees,
Sweet Freedom's song;
Let mortal tongues awake,
Let all that breathe partake,
Let rocks their silence break,–
The sound prolong.

Our fathers' God, to Thee,
Author of liberty,
To thee we sing;
Long may our land be bright
With Freedom's holy light;
Protect us by Thy might,
Great God, our King.

SAMUEL FRANCIS SMITH

DANIEL BOONE'S BENEDICTION

from The Life And Times of Col. Daniel Boone, by Edward S. Ellis,

Toward the close of the latter part of the century, Colonel Daniel Boone dictated his autobiography to a friend, and nothing can be more appropriate as an illustration of his character than these few closing words:

"My footsteps have often been marked with blood; two darling sons and a brother have I lost by savage hands, which have also taken forty valuable horses and cattle. Many dark and sleepless nights have I been a companion for owls, separated from the cheerful society of men, scorched by the summer's sun, and pinched by the winter's cold — an instrument ordained to settle the wilderness.

"What thanks, what ardent and ceaseless thanks are due to that all-superintending Providence which has turned a cruel war into peace, brought order out of confusion, made the fierce savages placid, and turned away their hostile weapons from our country.

"May the same almighty goodness banish the accursed monster, war, from all lands, with her hated associates, rapine and insatiable ambition!

"Let peace, descending from her native heaven, bid her olives spring amid the joyful nations; and plenty, in league with commerce, scatter blessings from her copious hand!"

Lord, let war's tempest cease,
Fold the whole world in peace
Under Thy wings.
Make all the nations one,
All hearts beneath the sun,
Till Thou shalt reign alone,
Great King of Kings.

Written for "America" by
Henry Wadsworth Longfellow

GOD grant that not only the love of liberty but a thorough knowledge of the rights of man may pervade all the nations of the earth, so that a philosopher may set his foot anywhere on its surface and say: "This is my country."

BENJAMIN FRANKLIN

merica is a tune; it must be sung together.

—GERALD STANLEY LEE

Americans are always moving on.

STEPHEN VINCENT BENÉT

The generation that subdued the wild land and broke up the virgin prairies inspires respect and compels admiration.

WILLA CATHER

We cross the prairie as of old
  The pilgrims crossed the sea,
To make the West, as they the East,
  The homestead of the free.

JOHN GREENLEAF WHITTIER

UNMANIFEST DESTINY

To what new gates, my country, far
  And unforseen of foe or friend,
Beneath what unexpected star,
  Compelled to what unchosen end.

Across the sea that knows no beach
  The Admiral of Nations guides
Thy blind obedient keels to reach
  The harbor where thy future rides!

The guns that spoke at Lexington
  Knew not that God was planning then
The trumpet word of Jefferson
  To bugle forth the rights of men.

To them that wept and cursed Bull Run,
  What was it but despair and shame?
Who saw behind the cloud the sun?
  Who knew that God was in the flame?

Had not defeat upon defeat,
  Disaster on disaster come,
The slave's emancipated feet
  Had never marched behind the drum.

There is a Hand that bends our deeds
  To mightier issues than we planned,
Each son that triumphs, each that bleeds,
  My country, serves Its dark command.

I do not know beneath what sky
  Nor on what seas shall be thy fate;
I only know it shall be high,
  I only know it shall be great.

—RICHARD HOVEY

THE UNITED STATES IN 1803 AFTER THE PURCHASE OF LOUISIANA, WITH BOUNDARY OF 1819 (§ 318)

West Florida, as far eastward as the Perdido River, was claimed as part of the purchase. In 1802 Congress added all that remained of the Northwest Territory (§ 237) to Indiana Territory (see map facing page 268). The "Oregon Country" was held jointly with Great Britain

THE CUMBERLAND OR NATIONAL ROAD

Through the influence of Henry Clay, who was called "the Father of the National Road," this work was begun in 1811 at Fort Cumberland, on the Potomac, Maryland. It was completed to Wheeling, on the Ohio River, 1820; to Zanesville, 1830; to Columbus, 1833; to Vandalia, Illinois, 1836. The proposed extension to Jefferson City, Missouri, was never carried out, since after 1836 the public interest began to center in the building of railways. Eventually the Federal Government handed over the National Road to the states through which it passed.

SCENE ON THE NATIONAL ROAD

PROMISED LAND

Idealism must always prevail on the frontier, for the frontier, whether geographical or intellectual, offers little hope to those who see things as they are. To venture into the wilderness, one must see it, not as it is, but as it will be. The frontier, being the possession of those only who see its future, is the promised land which cannot be entered save by those who have faith. America, having been such a Promised Land, is therefore inhabited by men of faith: idealism is ingrained in the character of the people.

CARL BECKER

FRONTIER PEOPLE

Much of our district was new settlements, formed and forming; hard, long rides, cabin parlors, straw beds and bedsteads, made out of barked saplings, and puncheon bedcords. But the people were kind and clever, proverbially so; showing the real pioneer or frontier hospitality. The men were a hardy, industrious, enterprising, game catching, and Indian driving set of men. The women were also hardy; they would think no hardship of turning out and helping their husbands raise their cabins, if need be; they would mount a horse and trot ten or fifteen miles to meeting, or to see the sick and minister to them, and home again the same day.

PETER CARTWRIGHT

HISTORICAL FOOTNOTE

The occasion had not been arranged and rehearsed as I suspect the sending of the first message over the Morse telegraph had been years before, for instead of that noble first telegraphic message—"What hath God wrought?"—the first message of the telephone was: "Mr. Watson, come here, I want you." Perhaps if Mr. Bell had realized that he was about to make a bit of history, he would have been prepared with a more sounding and interesting sentence.

THOMAS A. WATSON

"Gold is good in its place, but living, brave, patriotic men are Better Than Gold."

—Abraham Lincoln, November 10, 1864

Go West, young man, and grow up with the country.

HORACE GREELEY

To direct the genius and resources of our country to useful improvements, to the sciences, the arts, education, the amendment of the public mind and morals, in such pursuits lie real honor and the nation's glory.

ROBERT FULTON

HALL OF FAME INSCRIPTION

GOD, GIVE US MEN!

God, give us men! A time like this demands
Strong minds, great hearts, true faith and ready hands;
  Men whom the lust of office does not kill;
Men whom the spoils of office cannot buy;
  Men who possess opinions and a will;
Men who have honor; men who will not lie;
Men who can stand before a demagogue
  And damn his treacherous flatteries without winking!
Tall men, sun-crowned, who live above the fog
  In public duty and in private thinking;
For while the rabble, with their thumb-worn creeds,
Their large professions and their little deeds,
Mingle in selfish strife, lo! Freedom weeps,
Wrong rules the land and waiting Justice sleeps.

JOSIAH GILBERT HOLLAND

THE ALAMO

THE LAST MESSAGE FROM THE ALAMO

Commandancy of the Alamo, Bexar, February 24, 1836.—To the people of Texas and all Americans in the world. Fellow citizens and compatriots: I am besieged by a thousand or more of the Mexicans under Santa Anna. I have sustained a continual bombardment and cannonade for twenty-four hours and have not lost a man. The enemy has demanded a surrender at discretion; otherwise the garrison are to be put to the sword if the fort is taken. I have answered the demand with a cannon shot, and our flag still waves proudly from the walls. *I shall never surrender nor retreat.* Then, I call on you in the name of liberty, of patriotism, and everything dear to the American character, to come to our aid with all dispatch. The enemy is receiving reinforcements daily and will no doubt increase to three or four thousand in four or five days. If this call is neglected, I am determined to sustain myself as long as possible and die like a soldier who never forgets what is due to his own honor and that of our country. **VICTORY OR DEATH.**

—William Barret Travis
Lieutenant Colonel Commandant

P.S. The Lord is on our side. When the enemy appeared in sight we had not three bushels of corn. We have since found in deserted houses eighty or ninety bushels and got into the walls twenty or thirty head of beeves.

ALAMO INSCRIPTION

In memory of the heroes who sacrificed their lives at the Alamo, March 6, 1836, in the defense of Texas. They chose never to surrender nor retreat. These brave hearts, with flag still proudly waving, perished in the flames of immortality that their high sacrifice might lead to the founding of this Texas. From the fire that burned their bodies rose the eternal spirit of the sublime, heroic sacrifice which gave birth to an empire state.

SAN ANTONIO, TEXAS

From REPLY TO HAYNE

(JANUARY 27, 1830)

When my eyes shall be turned to behold for the last time the sun in heaven, may I not see him shining on the broken and dishonored fragments of a once glorious Union; on states dissevered, discordant, belligerent; on a land rent with civil feuds, or drenched, it may be, in fraternal blood! Let their last feeble and lingering glance rather behold the gorgeous ensign of the Republic, now known and honored throughout the earth, still full high advanced, its arms and trophies streaming in their original lustre, not a stripe erased or polluted, not a single star obscured, bearing for its motto no such miserable interrogatory as "What is all this worth?" nor those other words of delusion and folly, "Liberty first and Union afterwards"; but everywhere, spread all over in characters of living light, blazing on all its ample folds, as they float over the sea and over the land, and in every wind under the whole heavens, that other sentiment, dear to every true American heart—Liberty and Union, now and forever, one and inseparable!

DANIEL WEBSTER

Be sure you are right, then go ahead.

DAVID CROCKETT

They that can give up essential liberty to obtain a little temporary safety deserve neither liberty nor safety.

BENJAMIN FRANKLIN

Never take counsel of your fears.

"STONEWALL" JACKSON

The toll of greatness. The striking contrast between Lincoln's first known photograph and a portrait made on April 10, 1865, five days before his death, shows the depth of his ordeal and the toughness that enabled him to endure it. Fewer than 20 years had passed between the first picture and the last. In the final Gardner portrait his face is seamed, his eyes deep-sunk with weariness, but he is serene.

WHY WE LOVE LINCOLN

Let's skip all the things you've read about him, all the things you heard too often or too young.

Forget the face on the penny, the statue in Washington, the Emancipation Proclamation, the speech at Gettysburg. Forget the official things, and look at the big thing.

Why do we love this man, dead long before our time, yet dear to us as a father? What was there about Abraham Lincoln?

He came out of nowhere special—a cabin like any other out West. His folks were nobody special—pleasant, hard-working people like many others. Abe was a smart boy. He could do a good day's work on the farm. He told funny stories. He was strong and kind. He'd never try to cheat you, or fool you.

Young Abe worked at odd jobs and read law books at night. Eventually he found his way into local politics. And it was then that people, listening to his speeches, began to know there was something special about Abe Lincoln.

Abe talked about running a country as if it were something you could do. It was just a matter of people getting along.

He had nothing against anybody, rich or poor, who went his own way and let the other fellow go his. No matter how mixed up things got, Abe made you feel that the answer was somewhere among those old rules that everybody knows: no hurting, no cheating, no fooling.

Abe had a way of growing without changing. So it seemed perfectly natural to find him in the White House one day, paddling around in his slippers, putting his feet on a chair when he had a deep one to think about—the same Abe Lincoln he had always been, and yet the most dignified and the strongest and the steadiest man anybody had ever known.

And when the terrible war came that might have torn his country apart, no one doubted what Abe would do. He was a family man; he resolved to keep the American family together.

Abe Lincoln always did what most people would have done, said what most people wanted said, thought what most people thought when they stopped to think about it. He was everybody, grown a little taller—the warm and living proof of our American faith that greatness comes out of everywhere when it is free.

LOUIS REDMOND

From LINCOLN, THE MAN OF THE PEOPLE

The color of the ground was in him, the red
earth;
The smack and tang of elemental things:
The rectitude and patience of the cliff;
The goodwill of the rain that loves all
leaves;
The friendly welcome of the wayside well;
The courage of the bird that dares the sea;
The gladness of the wind that shakes the
corn;
The pity of the snow that hides all scars;
The secrecy of streams that make their way
Under the mountain to the rifted rock;
The tolerance and equity of light
That gives as freely to the shrinking flower
As to the great oak flaring to the wind—
To the grave's low hill as to the Matterhorn
That shoulders out the sky. Sprung from the
West,
He drank the valorous youth of a new world.
The strength of virgin forests braced his
mind,
The hush of spacious prairies stilled his
soul.
His words were oaks in acorns; and his
thoughts
Were roots that firmly gript the granite
truth.

EDWIN MARKHAM

FREE AT LAST

Promptly on the first day of the New Year (1863) the President issued his final proclamation. It set free forever all slaves held in the sections then fighting against the Union. Thousands of these slaves were then raising corn to feed the Confederate armies, and thousands more were working on Confederate fortifications. For the first time in the history of the war the government had struck secession at its root, and had dealt it a deathblow. The President declared that this "act of justice" was warranted "by the Constitution upon military necessity"; he invoked for it "the considerate judgment of mankind and the gracious favor of Almighty God."

REDUCED COPY OF A PART OF THE EMANCIPATION PROCLAMATION
(Jan. 1, 1863)

And by virtue of the power, and for the purpose aforesaid, I do order and declare that all persons held as slaves within said designated States, and parts of States, are, and henceforward shall be free; ------

And upon this act, sincerely believed to be an act of justice, warranted by the Constitution, upon military necessity, I invoke the considerate judgment of mankind, and the gracious favor of Almighty God.

(L.S.) Independence of the United States of America the eighty-seventh.

Abraham Lincoln

By the President;
William H. Seward,
Secretary of State

We run our memory back over the pages of history for about eighty-two years, and we discover that we were then a very small people, in point of numbers vastly inferior to what we are now, with a vastly less extent of country, with vastly less of everything we consider desirable among men.

We look upon the change as exceedingly advantageous to us and to our posterity, and we fix upon something that happened away back as in some way or other being connected with this rise of prosperity.

We find a race of men living, in that day, whom we claim as our fathers and grandfathers; they were iron men; they fought for the principle that they were contending for; and we understood by what they then did it has followed the degree of prosperity which we now enjoy has come to us. "We hold these truths to be self-evident, that all men are created equal." That is the electric cord in the Declaration that links the hearts of patriotic men as long as the love of freedom exists in the minds of men throughout the world.

ABRAHAM LINCOLN

We must have many Lincoln-hearted men.

VACHEL LINDSAY

I always consider the settlement of America with reverence and wonder as the opening of a grand scene and design in Providence for the illumination of the ignorant and the emancipation of the slavish part of mankind all over the world.

JOHN ADAMS

What constitutes the bulwark of our own liberty and independence? It is not our frowning battlements, our bristling sea coasts. . . Our reliance is in the love of liberty which God has planted in us. Our defense is in the spirit which prized liberty as the heritage of all men, in all lands everywhere.

—ABRAHAM LINCOLN

The highest test of the civilization of a race is its willingness to extend a helping hand to the less fortunate.

BOOKER T. WASHINGTON

Whoever serves his country well has no need of ancestors.

—Voltaire.

Executive Mansion
Washington, Nov 21, 1864

To Mrs Bixby, Boston, Mass,

Dear Madam.

I have been shown in the files of the War Department a statement of the Adjutant General of Massachusetts that you are the mother of five sons who have died gloriously on the field of battle. I feel how weak and fruitless must be any word of mine which should attempt to beguile you from the grief of a loss so overwhelming. But I cannot refrain from tendering you the consolation that may be found in the thanks of the republic they died to save. I pray that our Heavenly Father may assuage the anguish of your bereavement, and leave you only the cherished memory of the loved and lost, and the solemn pride that must be yours to have laid so costly a sacrifice upon the altar of freedom

Yours very sincerely and respectfully

A. Lincoln

On the walls of Brasenose College, Oxford University, England, this letter of the "rail-splitter" President hangs as a model of purest English, rarely, if ever, surpassed.

THE Gettysburg Address

November 19, 1863

FOUR SCORE and seven years ago our fathers brought forth on this continent a new nation, conceived in liberty, and dedicated to the proposition that all men are created equal.

Now we are engaged in a great civil war, testing whether that nation, or any nation so conceived and so dedicated, can long endure. We are met on a great battlefield of that war. We have come to dedicate a portion of that field as a final resting place for those who here gave their lives that that nation might live. It is altogether fitting and proper that we should do this.

But in a larger sense we cannot dedicate, we cannot consecrate, we cannot hallow this ground. The brave men, living and dead, who struggled here, have consecrated it far above our poor power to add or detract. The world will little note nor long remember what we say here, but it can never forget what they did here. It is for us, the living, rather, to be dedicated here to the unfinished work which they who fought here have thus far so nobly advanced. It is rather for us to be here dedicated to the great task remaining before us — that from these honored dead we take increased devotion to that cause for which they gave the last full measure of devotion; that we here highly resolve that these dead shall not have died in vain; that this nation, under God, shall have a new birth of freedom; and that government of the people, by the people, and for the people, shall not perish from the earth.

Abraham Lincoln's
GETTYSBURG ADDRESS

Four score and seven years ago our fathers brought forth, on this continent, a new nation, conceived in Liberty, and dedicated to the proposition that all men are created equal.

Now we are engaged in a great civil war, testing whether that nation, or any nation so conceived, and so dedicated, can long endure. We are met on a great battle-field of that war. We have come to dedicate a portion of that field, as a final resting-place for those who here gave their lives, that that nation might live. It is altogether fitting and proper that we should do this.

But, in a larger sense, we can not dedicate— we can not consecrate— we can not hallow— this ground. The brave men, living and dead, who struggled here, have consecrated it far above our poor power to add or detract. The world will little note, nor long remember what we say here, but it can never forget what they did here. It is for us the living, rather, to be dedicated here to the unfinished work which they who fought here have thus far so nobly advanced. It is rather for us to be here dedicated to the great task remaining before us— that from these honored dead we take increased devotion to that cause for which they here gave the last full measure of devotion— that we here highly resolve that these dead shall not have died in vain— that this nation, under God, shall have a new birth of freedom— and that government of the people, by the people, for the people, shall not perish from the earth.

Lincoln Goes to Gettysburg

Condensed from Redbook Magazine

Carl Sandburg

Author of "Abraham Lincoln—The Prairie Years," and "The War Years," etc.

WHEN Governor Curtin of Pennsylvania set aside November 19, 1863, for the dedication of a National Soldiers' Cemetery at Gettysburg, the only invitation President Lincoln received to attend the ceremonies was a printed circular.

The duties of orator of the day had fallen on Edward Everett. An eminent figure, perhaps the foremost of all American classical orators, he had been Governor of Massachusetts, Ambassador to Great Britain and President of Harvard. There were four published volumes of his orations. His lecture on Washington, delivered 122 times in three years, had in 1859 brought a fund of $58,000, which he gave for the purchase of Mount Vernon as a permanent shrine.

Serene, suave, handsomely venerable in his 69th year, Everett was a natural choice of the Pennsylvania commissioners, who gave him two months to prepare his address. The decision to invite Lincoln to speak was an afterthought. As one of the commissioners later wrote: "The question was raised as to his ability to speak upon such a solemn occasion; the invitation was not settled upon until about two weeks before the exercises were held."

In these dark days Lincoln was far from popular in many quarters. Some newspapers claimed that the President was going to make a stump speech over the graves of the Gettysburg dead as a political show. Thaddeus Stevens, Republican floor leader in the House, believed in '63 that Lincoln was a "dead card" in the political deck. He favored Chase for the next President, and hearing that Lincoln and Secretary of State Seward were going to Gettysburg, he commented: "The dead going to bury the dead."

*Selected from July **1936** issue of The Reader's Digest*

On the day before the ceremony a special train decorated with red-white-and-blue bunting stood ready to take the presidential party to Gettysburg. When his escort remarked that they had no time to lose, Lincoln said he felt like an Illinois man who was going to be hanged, and as the man passed along the road on the way to the gallows, the crowds kept pushing into the way and blocking passage. The condemned man at last called out: "Boys, you needn't be in such a hurry; there won't be any fun till I get there."

Reaching Gettysburg, Lincoln was driven to a private residence on the public square. The sleepy little country town was overflowing. Private homes were filled with notables and nondescripts. Hundreds slept on the floors of hotels. Bands blared till late in the night. When serenaders called on the President for a speech, he responded: "In my position it is sometimes important that I should not say foolish things." (A voice: "If you can help it.") "It very often happens that the only way to help it is to say nothing at all. Believing that is my present condition this evening, I must beg of you to excuse me from addressing you further." The crowd didn't feel it was much of a speech. They went next door with the band and blared for Seward.

Beset with problems attendant on the conduct of the war, Lincoln had had little time to prepare his address. About ten o'clock that night before the ceremony he sat down in his room to do more work on it. It was midnight or later when he went to sleep.

At least 15,000 people were on Cemetery Hill for the exercises next day when the procession from Gettysburg arrived afoot and horseback. The President's horse seemed small for him. One of the commissioners, riding just behind the President, noted that he sat erect and looked majestic to begin with, and then got to thinking so his body leaned forward, his arms hung limp and his head bent far down.

The parade had begun to move at eleven, and in 15 minutes it was over. But the orator of the day had not arrived. Bands played till noon. Mr. Everett arrived. On the platform sat state governors, Army officers, foreign ministers, Members of Congress, the President and his party.

When Edward Everett was introduced, he bowed low to Lincoln, then stood in silence before a crowd that stretched to limits that would test his voice. Around were the wheat fields, the meadows, the peach orchards and beyond, the contemplative blue ridge of a low mountain range. He had taken note of these in his prepared and rehearsed address. "Overlooking these broad fields now reposing from the labors of the waning year, the mighty Alleghenies dimly towering before us, the graves of our brethren beneath our feet, it is with hesitation that I raise my poor voice to break the eloquent silence of God and Nature."

He proceeded: "It was appointed by law in Athens–" and gave an extended sketch of the manner in which the Greeks cared for their dead who fell in battle. He gave an outline of how the war began, traversed decisive features of the three days' battles at Gettysburg, denounced the doctrine of state sovereignty, drew parallels from European history, and came to his peroration quoting Pericles on dead patriots: "The whole earth is the sepulcher of illustrious men." He spoke for an hour and 57 minutes. It was the effort of his life, and embodied the perfections of the school of oratory in which he had spent his career.

When the time came for Lincoln to speak he put on his steel-bowed glasses, rose, and holding in one hand the two sheets of paper at which he occasionally glanced, he delivered the address in his high-pitched and clear-carrying voice. A photographer bustled about with his equipment, but before he had his head under the hood for an exposure, the President had said "by the people and for the people," and the nick of time was past for a photograph. The nine sentences were spoken in five minutes, and the applause was merely formal–a tribute to the occasion, to the high office, by persons who had sat as an audience for three hours.

That evening Lincoln took the train back to Washington. He was weary, talked little, stretched out on the seats and had a wet towel laid across his forehead. He felt that about all he had given the audience was ordinary garden-variety dedicatory remarks. "That speech," he said, "was a flat failure, and the people are disappointed."

Much of the newspaper reaction was more condemnatory. The *Patriot and Union* of nearby Harrisburg took its fling: "The President acted without sense and without constraint in a panorama that was gotten up more for the benefit of his party than for the honor of the dead. . . . We pass over the silly remarks of the President; for the credit of the nation we are willing that the veil of oblivion shall be dropped over them and that they shall no more be repeated or thought of." And the Chicago *Times* fumed: "The cheek of every American must tingle with shame as he reads the silly, flat and dish-watery utterances of the man who has to be pointed out to intelligent foreigners as the President of the United States." Wrote the correspondent of the London *Times*, "Anything more dull and commonplace it would not be easy to produce."

A reporter for the Chicago *Tribune,* however, telegraphed a prophetic sentence: "The dedicatory remarks of President Lincoln will live among the annals of man." The Philadelphia *Evening Bulletin* said thousands who would not read the elaborate oration of Mr. Everett would read the President's few words, "and not many will do it without a moistening of the eye and a swelling of the heart." And a writer in *Harper's Weekly:* "The oration by Mr. Everett was smooth and cold. . . . The few words of the President were from the heart to the heart. They cannot be read, even, without kindling emotion. 'The world will little note nor long remember what we say here, but it can never forget what they did here.' It was as simple and felicitous and earnest a word as was ever spoken."

Everett's opinion of the speech, written in a note to Lincoln the next day, was more than mere courtesy. "I should be glad if I could flatter myself that I came as near to the central idea of the occasion in two hours as you did in two minutes." Lincoln's immediate reply: "In our respective parts you could not have been excused to make a short address, nor I a long one. I am pleased to know that, in your judgment, the little I did say was not entirely a failure."

FONDLY do we hope–fervently do we pray–that this mighty scourge of war may speedily pass away.

Yet if God wills that it continue until all the wealth piled by the bondsman's two hundred and fifty years of unrequited toil shall be sunk, and until every drop of blood drawn with the lash shall be paid by another drawn with the sword, as was said three thousand years ago, so still it must be said, "the judgments of the Lord are true and righteous altogether."

With malice toward none; with charity for all; with firmness in the right, as God gives us to see the right, let us strive on to finish the work we are in; to bind up the nation's wounds; to care for him who shall have borne the battle, and for his widow and his orphan–to do all which may achieve and cherish a just and a lasting peace among ourselves and with all nations.

Abraham Lincoln

BREVITY IS A VIRTUE

Abraham Lincoln's only autobiography was written in 1848 at the request of Charles Lanman, who was then making up his "Dictionary of Congress," and had asked Mr. Lincoln for a sketch of his life. The following is Abraham Lincoln's written reply: "Born February 12, 1809, in Hardin County, Kentucky. Education, defective. Profession, lawyer. Have been a captain of volunteers in the Black Hawk War. Postmaster at a very small office. Four times a member of the Illinois legislature. And was a member of the lower House of Congress. Yours, etc., A. Lincoln."

The frontier, for all its savage brutal habits, had created, if only now and then, characters that rose superior to destiny.

ELLEN GLASGOW

The Frontiersman

The suns of summer seared his skin;
The cold his blood congealed;
The forest giants blocked his way;
The stubborn acres' yield
He wrenched from them by dint of arm,
And grim old Solitude
Broke bread with him and shared his cot
Within the cabin rude.
The gray rocks gnarled his massive hands;
The north wind shook his frame;
The wolf of hunger bit him oft;
The world forgot his name;
But mid the lurch and crash of trees,
Within the clearing's span
Where now the bursting wheat-heads dip,
The Fates turned out—a man!

—*Richard Wightman*

That patriotism, which, catching its inspiration from the immortal God, animates and prompts to deeds of self-sacrifice, of valor, of devotion, and of death itself—that is public virtue, that is the sublimest of all public virtues.

HENRY CLAY

Democracy means not "I am as good as you are" but "You are as good as I am."

THEODORE PARKER

He leaves for America's history and biography, so far, not only its most dramatic reminiscence—he leaves, in my opinion, the greatest, best, most characteristic, artistic, moral personality.

WALT WHITMAN

It is the great boon of such characters as Mr. Lincoln's, that they reunite what God has joined together and man has put asunder. In him was vindicated the greatness of real goodness and the goodness of real greatness.

PHILLIPS BROOKS

Robert Edward Lee, general in chief of the Southern armies and the greatest figure of the Confederacy. A West Point graduate who served under General Winfield Scott in the Mexican War, Lee had no sympathy for secession. But he was a loyal Virginian. Offered command of the Union armies early in 1861, he told Francis P. Blair, Sr., "If I owned . . . four million slaves . . . I would sacrifice them all to the Union. But how can I draw my sword against Virginia?"

Ulysses Simpson Grant, Lieutenant General in the Army of the United States. This rank, which had been held before only by George Washington, was revived by act of Congress in February 1864, and Grant received his commission from Lincoln's own hand at the White House in early March. This photograph of Grant was made at Cold Harbor, Virginia, in June 1864, when hard contests in the Wilderness, at Spotsylvania and at North Anna were already behind him. His grinding pressure on Lee's army—costly though it was in lives—was paying off.

No terms except an unconditional and immediate surrender can be accepted. I propose to move immediately upon your works.

I am sir, very respectfully
your obt. svt.
U. S. Grant
Brig. Gen

GENERAL ULYSSES S. GRANT'S UNCONDITIONAL SURRENDER LETTER

7th Apl '65

Genl

I have recd your note
of this date. Though not enter
taining the opinion you express
of the hopelessness of further resis
-tance on the part of the Army
of N. Va — I reciprocate your
desire to avoid useless effusion
of blood, & therefore before Consider
ing your proposition ask
the terms you will offer on
Condition of its Surrender

Very respt your Obt Servt

R E Lee
Genl

Lt Genl U. S. Grant
Commd Armies of the U. States

LEE'S LETTER OF SURRENDER

Federal troops in front of Wilmer McLean's house at Appomattox Court House, Virginia. It was in McLean's parlor that General Robert E. Lee surrendered his army to Ulysses S. Grant on Palm Sunday, April 9, 1865. Grant's terms were humane, and Lee told him, "This will have a very happy effect on my army." The war was over when Timothy O'Sullivan took this photograph, and the Northern soldiers were relaxed, joking, enjoying peace, victory, life and the warm spring sunshine of Virginia.

THE CHARACTER OF LEE

He possessed every virtue of the great commanders, without their vices. He was a foe without hate; a friend without treachery; a private citizen without wrong; a neighbor without reproach; a Christian without hypocrisy, and a man without guilt.

He was a Caesar without his ambition; a Frederick without his tyranny; a Napoleon without his selfishness; and a Washington without his reward.

He was obedient to authority as a servant, and loyal in authority as a true king.

He was gentle as a woman in life; modest and pure as a virgin in thought; watchful as a Roman vestal in duty; submissive to law as Socrates, and grand in battle as Achilles.

JOHN WILLIAM JONES

ROBERT E. LEE

The man was loved, the man was idolized,
The man had every just and noble gift.
He took great burdens and he bore them
well,
Believed in God but did not preach too much,
Believed and followed duty first and last
With marvellous consistency and force,
Was a great victor, in defeat as great,
No more, no less, always himself in both,
Could make men die for him but saved his
men
Whenever he could save them—was most
kind
But was not disobeyed—was a good father,
A loving husband, a considerate friend.

STEPHEN VINCENT BENÉT
From JOHN BROWN'S BODY

The ideal state is that in which an injury done to the least of its citizens is an injury done to all.

—SOLON

If it were my destiny to die for the cause of liberty, I would die upon the tomb of the Union, the American flag as my winding sheet.

ANDREW JOHNSON

"The Worst Day of My Life"

Robert E. Lee

It was Palm Sunday. For seven days and nights Robert E. Lee had led his disintegrating Army of Northern Virginia west. Behind him was Ulysses S. Grant's Army of the Potomac and the Army of the James, several times as large and ravenous with the scent of victory.

Swarms of Phil Sheridan's cavalry had swept ahead of Lee's weary veterans, cutting the railroad line that might have carried them to safety, capturing tons of precious supplies. Again and again, saber-swinging horsemen hacked and smashed at Lee's line of march, forcing his exhausted men to fight them off.

By Saturday, April 8, there were only two small divisions capable of battle. Around them in the woods and along the roads toward Appomattox Court House swarmed thousands of fellow soldiers, demoralized, searching for food, staying with the army only because Robert E. Lee still led them. But at Appomattox Lee found his last road blocked by Sheridan's cavalry.

At dawn on Palm Sunday, the Confederate infantry under fiery Bryan Grimes, a Brigadier General only six weeks, probed the Northern lines and found them deep and solid. Lee watched the fighting through his glasses, then said to his staff, "There is nothing left for me to do but go and see General Grant—and I would rather die a thousand deaths." On April 7, Grant had first written Lee, inviting him to surrender, but Lee still had hopes of leading his army westward to safety.

Tall, bearded General James ("Old Pete") Longstreet, the general Lee trusted most, rode up. Longstreet later recalled how fine Lee looked. His uniform, the only one he had left, was new, and he was wearing a pair of gold spurs. "At first approach, his compact figure appeared as a man in the flush vigor of 40 summers, but as I drew near the handsome apparel and brave bearing failed to conceal his profound depression."

"Can the sacrifice of the army help the cause in other quarters?" Longstreet asked.

"I think not," Lee said.

"Then," Longstreet said, "your situation speaks for itself."

Lee asked his brilliant artillery general, E. P. Alexander, what he thought. "We have two alternatives," Alexander said. "We must surrender or scatter in the woods and bushes and rally to General Johnston in North Carolina . . . Scattering would be best."

There were other officers who agreed with Alexander. But Lee decided against it. "The men would have no rations, be under no discipline . . . They'd have to rob and plunder." Lee had earlier told his staff, "It is our duty to live. What will become of the women and children of the South if we are not here to protect them?"

Lee's decision was just in time. The long blue ranks were ready to advance. Sheridan rode up and down the line: "Now smash 'em, I tell you! Smash 'em!" Off to the right the whole cavalry corps of the Army of the Potomac formed, sun gleaming on flags and sabers. Below, one Federal officer remembered afterwards, in the Rebel lines it seemed there were more battle flags than soldiers, so small were the Southern regiments. Another minute and the Army of Northern Virginia would have vanished.

Then out of the Confederate lines rode an officer with a staff in his hand, a white flag fluttering from the end of it. To the Union officer who met him he handed a letter from General Lee to General Grant.

Unfortunately, Grant was far behind his lines, so Lee's offer did not reach him until about 11 a.m. when he and his staff were eight or nine miles east of Appomattox Court House resting their horses in a newly cleared field. Sylvanus Cadwallader, a newspaperman who had followed Grant in the field for three years, recalled his expression. "There was no exultation manifested—no sign of joy—and instead of flushing from excitement he clenched his teeth, compressed his lips, and became very pale."

Grant read the letter, then had it read aloud by an aide. There was a moment of silence. "No one looked his comrade in the face," Cadwallader recalled. "Finally Colonel Duff, chief of artillery, sprang upon a log, waved his hat and proposed three cheers. A feeble hurrah came from a few throats, when all broke down in tears and but little was said for several minutes." Grant summoned his military secretary, Colonel Ely Parker, a giant full-blooded Iroquois known as "The Indian." Quickly Grant dictated an answer stating his willingness to meet Lee.

Colonel Orville Babcock of Grant's staff carried the reply through the Confederate lines. The Southern general had meanwhile selected a two-story brick farmhouse owned by Major Wilmer McLean, who had moved to Appomattox from Manassas after his property had been smashed and destroyed in the battles of Bull Run. As Lee's aide Charles Marshall recalled it, the three men sat down in McLean's parlor and "talked in the most friendly and affable way."

Grant rode up with a dozen members of his staff. If Lee had "dreaded" the interview, Grant was almost as apprehensive. "When I had left camp that morning I had not expected so soon the result that was then

Reprinted from THIS WEEK MAGAZINE / July 4, 1965

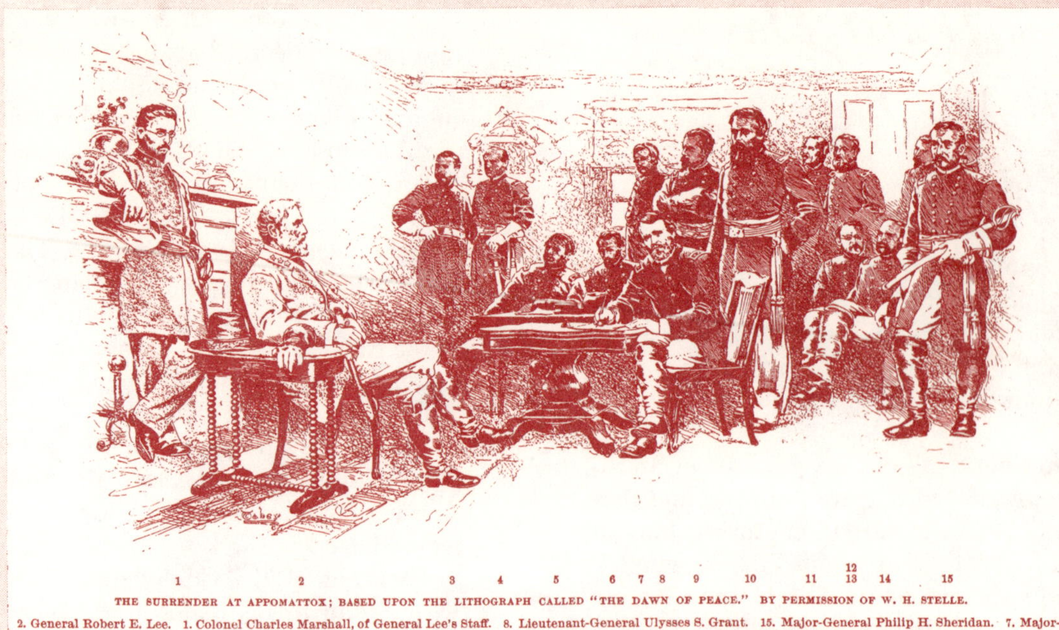

THE SURRENDER AT APPOMATTOX; BASED UPON THE LITHOGRAPH CALLED "THE DAWN OF PEACE." BY PERMISSION OF W. H. STELLE.

2. General Robert E. Lee. 1. Colonel Charles Marshall, of General Lee's Staff. 8. Lieutenant-General Ulysses S. Grant. 15. Major-General Philip H. Sheridan. 7. Major-General Edward O. C. Ord. 14. Brevet Major-General Rufus Ingalls. 10. Brigadier-General John A. Rawlins, Chief-of-Staff; other members of General Grant's Staff: 4. Major-General Seth Williams. 12. Brevet Major-General John G. Barnard. 9. Colonel Horace Porter. 3. Colonel Orville E. Babcock. 5. Colonel Ely S. Parker. 6. Colonel Theodore S. Bowers. 11. Colonel Frederick T. Dent. 13. Colonel Adam Badeau.

Then Grant scribbled in pencil in his order book on a small table that Parker brought him. Toward the end, he paused and glancing at Lee's dress sword said, *"This will not embrace the sidearms of the officers nor their private horses or baggage."*

Lee asked only one concession, that the Southern cavalrymen and artillerymen be allowed to retain their horses, which they owned privately. Grant was not aware of this arrangement. At first he said that the terms did not allow it.

"No," Lee said, *"I see the terms do not allow it. That is clear."*

There was a long silence. Lee's face, according to General Porter, "showed plainly that he was quite anxious to have this concession made." Finally, Grant said, *"I will arrange it in this way: I will not change the terms as they are written, but I will instruct the officers to let all the men who claim to own a horse or mule take the animals home with them to work their little farms."*

"This will have the best possible effect upon my men," Lee said. *"It will be very gratifying and will do much toward conciliating our people."*

When Parker started to make a draft of the terms, the Indian discovered he was out of ink and had to borrow some from Lee's aide, Charles Marshall, who in turn wrote a brief acceptance for Lee to sign.

Grant then introduced his officers to Lee. When he shook hands with Parker, Lee said, *"I am glad to see one real American here."*

"We are all Americans," Parker said.

Lee told Grant he had 1,500 Union prisoners, but neither the prisoners nor the captors had any food.

taking place and consequently was in rough garb. I was without a sword as I usually was when on horseback on the field, and wore a soldier's blouse for a coat with the shoulder straps of my rank to indicate to the army who I was."

Lee rose as Grant entered and the conqueror said, *"I met you once before, General Lee, while we were serving in Mexico when you came over from General Scott's headquarters to visit Garland's brigade. I have always remembered your appearance and I think I should have recognized you anywhere."*

Lee replied, *"Yes, I know I met you on that occasion and I have often tried to recollect how you looked but I have never been able to recall a single feature."*

Union officers crowded onto the porch. The room filled with generals. Grant in the center of the room faced Lee by the front window with Marshall. It was by now 1:30 p.m.

Conversation wandered. Grant was ill at ease. "What General Lee's feelings were I do not know," he later wrote, ". . . but my own feelings . . . were sad and depressed."

Lee finally said, *"I suppose, General Grant, that the object of our meeting is fully understood. I asked to see you to ascertain on what terms you would receive the surrender of my army."*

Grant's answer was concise: "*. . . The officers and men surrendered to be paroled and disqualified from taking up arms again until properly exchanged and all arms, ammunition and supplies to be delivered up as cashiered property."*

"Those are about the conditions I expected," Lee said.

Michael R. Morgan, the assistant Commissary General, asked how many men Lee had in his army. "Our books are lost," Lee said, "our organizations are broken up. The companies are mostly commanded by noncommissioned officers. We have nothing but what we have on our backs."

"Say twenty-five thousand men?" Morgan asked.

"Yes," Lee said, "say twenty-five thousand."

Morgan promptly ordered three days' rations sent into the Confederate lines. "Fresh beef, salt, hard bread, coffee, and sugar."

There was a little more scattered conversation and Lee rose, shook hands with Grant and left the room, followed by Marshall. It was 4 p.m.

Outside on the porch, all the Federal officers snapped to salute. Lee returned it "mechanically but courteously," in the memory of one observer. His orderly brought the famed gray horse Traveller to the porch. As he mounted, one watcher recalled "there broke unguardedly from his lips a long, low, deep sigh, almost a groan in its intensity." Grant left a few minutes later.

Poor Wilmer McLean then had to stand by while the remaining Union officers auctioned and looted his furniture for souvenirs. When McLean refused, they forced money into his hands and took them anyway. Within the hour, the house was stripped almost bare.

Lee spent the rest of the day in an orchard beneath the shade of a tree where, in the words of Captain W. W. Blackford, "he paced backwards and forwards looking like a caged lion." A number of Union officers came to see him. Many were friends from the old army but Lee shook hands with none of them, and would exchange only a few brief words.

Near sunset, he mounted Traveller again and rode to his headquarters. All down the line men streamed from their bivouacs for a last salute, tears mingling with cheers. Lee rode with his hat off, tears streaming down his own cheeks. At his tent he turned to the men and said, "*Boys, I have done the best I could for you. Go home now and if you make as good citizens as you have soldiers, you will do well and I shall always be proud of you. Goodbye and God bless you all.*"

That evening the Federals poured into the Confederate camp, generously sharing rations and whiskey with the half-starved Southerners. From generals to privates there was everywhere evidence that the terrible wounds of war might be healed more swiftly than most men had dared to hope. When someone told Grant that he should have held Lee and his generals for trial instead of paroling them, the stumpy victor said quietly, "I'll keep the terms no matter who's opposed. But Lincoln is sure to be on my side."

—Thomas J. Fleming

FAREWELL TO THE ARMY OF NORTHERN VIRGINIA

After four years of arduous service, marked by unsurpassed courage and fortitude, the Army of Northern Virginia has been compelled to yield to overwhelming numbers and resources.

I need not tell the survivors of so many hard-fought battles who have remained steadfast to the last that I have consented to this result from no distrust of them; but feeling that valor and devotion could accomplish nothing that could compensate for the loss that would have attended the continuance of the contest, I determined to avoid the useless sacrifice of those whose past services have endeared them to their countrymen. By the terms of the agreement, officers and men can return to their homes and remain until exchanged.

You may take with you the satisfaction that proceeds from the consciousness of duty faithfully performed, and I earnestly pray that a merciful God will extend to you his blessing and protection.

With an unceasing admiration of your constancy and devotion to your country, and a grateful remembrance of your kind and generous consideration of myself, I bid you all an affectionate farewell.

ROBERT E. LEE

Let reverence for the laws be breathed by every American mother to the lisping babe that prattles on her lap; let it be taught in schools, in seminaries, and in colleges; let it be written in primers, spelling books, and in almanacs; let it be preached from the pulpit, proclaimed in legislative halls, and enforced in courts of justice. And, in short, let it become the political religion of the nation; and let the old and the young, the rich and the poor, the grave and the gay of all sexes and tongues and colors and conditions, sacrifice unceasingly upon its altars.

ABRAHAM LINCOLN

They Also Served

Poet SIDNEY LANIER fought as a private in the 2nd Georgia Battalion during the Seven Days' Battles near Richmond. In November 1862 he was captured on a Confederate blockade-runner and imprisoned at Point Lookout, Maryland. Sixteen years after the war he died from tuberculosis contracted while in prison.

New England poet ALBERT PIKE commanded the Confederate Department of Indian Territory. He wrote the stanzas of the popular Southern version of *Dixie*, a tune which originated not in the South, but in New York City during the 1850's.

At the battle of the Monocacy in 1864 Union General LEW WALLACE, author of *Ben-Hur*, commanded the force defending Washington against General Jubal Early's attack. After the war he served as Governor of New Mexico and Minister to Turkey.

When the Marion Rangers organized in 1861, SAMUEL CLEMENS (Mark Twain) joined as a lieutenant, but he left this Missouri Company before it was mustered into Confederate service, having fired only one hostile shot during the war.

Confederate private HENRY MORTON STANLEY, of "Doctor Livingston, I presume" fame, survived a bloody charge at Shiloh only to be taken prisoner. Later he joined the Union ranks and finished the war in Yankee blue.

ANDREW CARNEGIE was a young man in his mid-twenties when he left his position as Superintendent of the Pittsburgh Division, Pennsylvania Railroad to pitch in with workers rebuilding the rail line from Annapolis to Washington. Later in 1861 he was given the position of superintendent of military railways and government telegraph.

HENRY A. DUPONT, grandson of the DuPont industries founder, was awarded the Congressional Medal of Honor for gallantry at the battle of Cedar Creek in October 1864. Captain DuPont, who had graduated from West Point at the head of his class in 1861, went on to serve as United States Senator from Delaware.

ELIAS HOWE presented each field and staff officer of the 5th Massachusetts Regiment with a stallion fully equipped for service. Later, he volunteered as a private, and when the State failed to pay his unit, he met the regimental payroll with his own money.

At the age of 15 GEORGE WESTINGHOUSE ran away from home and joined the Union Army. Neither he nor Elias Howe rose to officer rank, but both are today in the Hall of Fame for their achievements—the air brake and the sewing machine.

In 1861 CORNELIUS VANDERBILT presented a high-speed side-wheel steamer to the United States Navy. At the time, there were less than 50 ships in active naval service. The cruiser, named the *Vanderbilt*, captured three blockade-runners during the war and in 1865 participated in the bombardment and amphibious assault on Fort Fisher. The Federal Navy at that time had grown to a fleet of more than 550 steam-powered ships.

Admiral GEORGE DEWEY, of Manila Bay fame, served as a young lieutenant under Admiral Farragut during the attack on Port Hudson in 1863. His ship was the only one lost in the engagement.

Colonel CHRISTOPHER C. ("Kit") CARSON commanded the 1st New Mexico Volunteers (Union), and campaigned against the Comanche, Navajo, and Apache Indians during the Civil War. In 1866 he was promoted to brigadier general.

In his mid-teens JESSE JAMES joined the Confederate raiders led by William Quantrill. The famous "Dead or alive" reward for Jesse in 1882 was issued by an ex-Confederate officer, Governor Thomas T. Crittenden of Missouri.

HAVING HARD TIMES?

There is a certain businessman who, whenever someone comes into his office bemoaning his misfortunes in business, love, or life in general, takes him aside and invites him to study a framed handlettered sign hanging on the wall. It reads:

"Failed in business—'31
Defeated for Legislature—'32
Failed in business again—'33
Elected to Legislature—'34
Sweetheart died—'35
Suffered nervous breakdown—'36
Defeated for Speaker—'38
Defeated for Elector—'40
Defeated for Congress—'43
Elected to Congress—'46
Defeated for Congress—'48
Defeated for Senate—'55
Defeated for Vice President—'56
Defeated for Senate—'58
Elected President of the United States —'60

And the name beneath this record of misfortune, crowned by final success? ABRAHAM LINCOLN.

Andrew Johnson's Impeachment

The President, in disregard of the Tenure of Office Act, which he considered unconstitutional, resolved to remove Secretary Stanton, with whom he had long been at swords' points. He accordingly (August 5, 1867) sent the Secretary this brief note. "Sir: Public considerations of a high character constrain me to say that your resignation as Secretary of War will be accepted." Mr. Stanton, in his almost equally brief reply, said: "Sir: . . . I have the honor to say that public considerations of a high character, which alone have induced me to continue at the head of this department, constrain me not to resign the office of Secretary of War before the next meeting of Congress." Senator Sumner telegraphed to Stanton this one emphatic word, "Stick!" and "stick" he did.

The President thereupon suspended the Secretary from office, but Congress promptly reinstated him. He then ordered the Secretary to resign. Instead of doing so, Mr. Stanton sent the order to the House of Representatives. Thereupon that body resolved by a vote of 128 to 47 to impeach the President for "high crimes and misdemeanors." The offenses with which he was charged were: (1) the removal of Secretary Stanton in direct violation of the Tenure of Office Act; (2) commanding General Emory not to obey the law requiring all military orders to be issued through General Grant; (3) attempting to excite the resentment of the people against Congress by declaring that it was not a true Congress and that the President was not bound by its laws.

The impeachment trial began the last of March (1868) before fifty-four senators, representing twenty-seven states; Chief Justice Chase presided. It ended May 26. Thirty-five senators voted "guilty" and nineteen "not guilty." A two-thirds vote was required to secure conviction; the President, therefore, escaped removal by the narrow margin of a single vote.

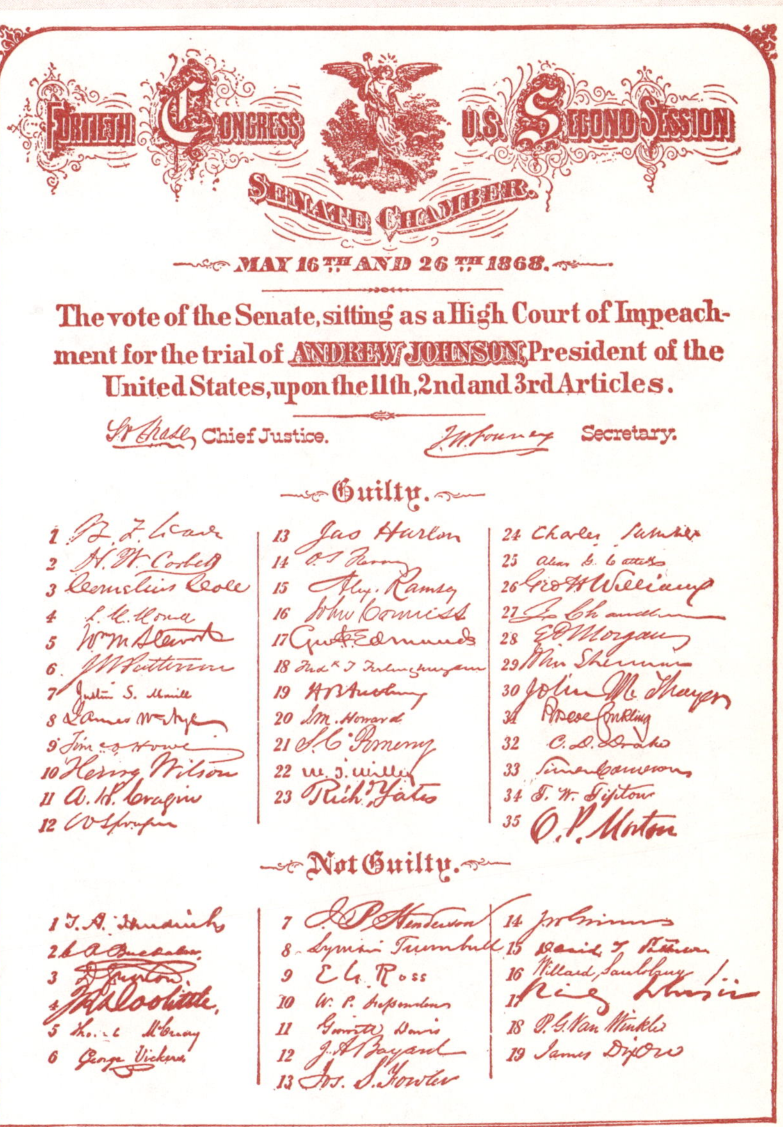

FORTIETH CONGRESS U.S. SECOND SESSION

SENATE CHAMBER.

MAY 16TH AND 26TH 1868.

The vote of the Senate, sitting as a High Court of Impeachment for the trial of ANDREW JOHNSON, President of the United States, upon the 11th, 2nd and 3rd Articles.

Chief Justice. Secretary.

Guilty.

Not Guilty.

VOTE ON THE IMPEACHMENT TRIAL

INSTITUTIONS MUST KEEP PACE WITH THE TIMES

A quotation from the writings of Thomas Jefferson

I AM not an advocate for frequent changes in laws and constitutions. But laws and institutions must go hand in hand with the progress of the human mind as that becomes more developed, more enlightened, as new discoveries are made, new truths discovered and manners and opinions change; with the change of circumstance, institutions must advance also to keep pace with the times. We might as well require a man to wear still the coat which fitted him when a boy, as civilized society to remain ever under the regimen of their barbarous ancestors.

I have sworn upon the altar of God eternal hostility against every form of tyranny over the mind of man.

Freedom of religion; freedom of the press; freedom of person under the protection of the habeas corpus.

—*First inaugural address,* THOMAS JEFFERSON

History interposes with evidence that tyranny and wrong lead inevitably to decay; that freedom and right, however hard may be the struggle, always prove resistless.

GEORGE BANCROFT

We have lived long, gentlemen, but this [Louisiana Purchase] is the noblest work of our lives.

—*Robert R. Livingston*

Sweet Land of Liberty

THE AMERICAN'S CREED

I believe in the United States of America as a government of the people, by the people, for the people; whose just powers are derived from the consent of the governed; a democracy in a republic; a sovereign nation of many sovereign states; a perfect union, one and inseparable; established upon those principles of freedom, equality, and humanity for which American patriots sacrificed their lives and fortunes. I, therefore, believe it is my duty to my country to love it, to support its constitution, to obey its laws, to respect its flag, and to defend it against all enemies.

WILLIAM TYLER PAGE

ADOPTED BY CONGRESS (1918)

Bartholdi, left, and Edouard de Laboulaye

How Miss Liberty Came to America

By John Mulligan

Americans, here's a Fourth of July story as patriotic as a Sousa march and as colorful as fireworks.

It's about the man who first thought of the Statue of Liberty—the almost forgotten Edouard de Laboulaye.

His story begins on a summer night in 1865 at his country "retraite" in Glatigny, just outside the Paris suburb of Versailles.

Laboulaye's retraite was "un coin d' Amerique"—a corner of America—where the law professor and historian surrounded himself with his lifetime and pastime, the United States, and where his many American friends felt the tug of home.

Portraits of Jefferson and Franklin stared down, shelves were lined with books on America, many of them by Laboulaye, including a translation of Franklin's autobiography, and their host sadly showed them his treasure, a letter on Executive Mansion stationery signed "A. Lincoln."

Chance Purchase

Laboulaye, a devout Catholic who had written that liberty was "the gospel's daughter, the sister of justice and mercy, the mother of equality, abundance and peace," said his affection for America began with the chance purchase at a Seine bookstall of the works of a Boston Protestant theologian, Dr. William Ellery Channing.

Others felt he may have been inspired at 19 when he saw the aged Lafayette spurring a white horse toward the barricades of Paris in the Revolution of 1830.

★★★★★★★★★★★★★★★★★★★★★★★★★★★★★

On that night in Glatigny, some of France's best minds, having enjoyed Laboulaye's cuisine and cellar, argued about the ingratitude of nations over cafe noir and cigars as dark.

One mentioned America. Another, a young Alsatian sculptor, Frederic Auguste Bartholdi, was to remember later that Laboulaye quickly interjected that "America and France are sisters," tried by fire in the days when Lafayette, Rochambeau and other French volunteers flocked to the American cause.

Something Remains

"When hearts have beaten together, something always remains among nations as among individuals," Laboulaye continued, "there you have the basis of American feeling for the French—an indestructable basis."

"The feeling honors the Americans as well as us," Laboulaye said, adding the words that would change Bartholdi's life, "and, if a memorial should rise in the United States as a memorial to their independence, I think it only natural if it were built by united effort—a common work of both our nations."

Six years would pass before the friends of Glatigny discussed the "memorial" again. The disastrous Franco-Prussian war was over. The grieving Bartholdi's native Alsace was lost to Germany and he gladly left for the New World at Laboulaye's bidding, to try to interest Americans in a joint venture for a "statue of liberty."

Chose the Island

On a June day in 1871, as the SS *Pereire* steamed into New York, Bartholdi quickly sketched a water-color of his colossal "La Liberte Eclairant le Monde"—liberty enlightening the world—and even chose the island where she would stand.

Keeping Laboulaye informed, Bartholdi toured America; out to San Francisco, down to the White House, up to the home of Henry Wadsworth Longfellow in Nahant, Mass.

The poet remembered Bartholdi "has a plan for creating a bronze colossus of Bedloe's Island in New York Harbor—a Statue of Liberty, to serve as a lighthouse. It is a grand plan: I hope it will strike the New Yorkers."

Across the ocean, the American press took up the cause. Laboulaye was thrilled to learn that on Washington's Birthday, 1877, Congress authorized a future President to accept the completed statue.

First Rivet

In 1881, on the centennial of Cornwallis' surrender to the Americans and French at Yorktown, U.S. Minister Levi P. Morton drove the first rivet into the foot of Miss Liberty as she began to be mounted, piece-by-piece, on a towering frame designed by Gustave Eiffel, who would later create Paris' landmark.

On July 4, 1884, Morton would accept Lady Liberty for America, and on Oct. 28, 1886, President Cleveland and Bartholdi would unveil her in New York Harbor.

But Laboulaye would witness neither triumph. He died at 71 on May 25, 1883.

Ambassador Morton attended the requiem and walked bare-headed behind the coffin to Pere Lachaise cemetery after cabling Washington: "He was a devoted friend of our country and our government; although he never crossed the ocean, he knew America and American history, I dare say, better than many Americans."

THE BALD EAGLE

The figure of this noble bird is well known throughout the civilized world, emblazoned as it is on our national standard, which waves in the breeze of every clime, bearing to distant lands the remembrance of a great people living in a state of peaceful freedom. May that peaceful freedom last for ever! The great strength, daring and cool courage of the White-headed Eagle, joined to his unequalled power of flight, render him highly conspicuous among his brethren. To these qualities did he add a generous disposition towards others, he might be looked up to as a model of nobility. The ferocious, overbearing and tyrannical temper which is ever and anon displaying itself in his actions, is, nevertheless, best adapted to his state, and was wisely given him by the Creator to enable him to perform the office assigned to him.

JOHN JAMES AUDUBON

The torch held high in the hand of liberty scatters the darkness of natural inequality and reveals the royal kinship of all men in God.

ROBERT I. GANNON

THE NEW COLOSSUS

Not like the brazen giant of Greek fame,
With conquering limbs astride from
land to land,
Here at our sea-washed, sunset gates shall
stand
A mighty woman with a torch, whose flame
Is the imprisoned lightning, and her name
Mother of Exiles. From her beacon-hand
Glows world-wide welcome;
her mild eyes command
The air-bridged harbor that twin cities frame.
"Keep, ancient lands, your storied pomp!"
cries she
With silent lips. "Give me your tired,
your poor,
Your huddled masses yearning to breathe
free,
The wretched refuse of your teeming shore.
Send these, the homeless, tempest-tost to me,
I lift my lamp beside the golden door!"

This tablet, with her Sonnet to the Bartholdi Statue of Liberty engraved upon it, is placed upon these walls in loving memory of
EMMA LAZARUS
Born in New York City, July 22, 1849
Died November 18, 1887

AMERICANISM

There is one quality which we must bring to the solution of every problem—that is, an intense and fervid Americanism. We shall never be successful over the dangers that confront us; we shall never achieve true greatness, nor reach the lofty ideal which the founders and preservers of our mighty Federal Republic have set before us, unless we are Americans in heart and soul, in spirit and purpose, keenly alive to the responsibility implied in the very name of American, and proud beyond measure of the glorious privilege of bearing it.

THEODORE ROOSEVELT

OATH OF NATURALIZED CITIZENS

I hereby declare, on oath, that I absolutely and entirely renounce and abjure all allegiance and fidelity to any foreign prince, potentate, state, or sovereignty of whom or which I have heretofore been a subject or citizen; that I will support and defend the Constitution and laws of the United States of America against all enemies, foreign and domestic; that I will bear true faith and allegiance to the same; and that I take this obligation freely without any mental reservation or purpose of evasion; so help me God. In acknowledgment whereof I have hereunto affixed my signature.

I am doubly an American, because I am foreign-born. It may be that the native-born Americans take America for granted. Foreign-born Americans like myself do not take America for granted. We look upon American citizenship as the most precious and sacred of boons. We understand what it is that we have left behind us—of denial of the freedoms of man—and we know what it is that has come to be our high destiny, to be a sharer in Amerian freedom, to be a bearer of American responsibility, to be a devotee of the American Democracy, to use American freedom not for one's own advantage but for the service of the American Democracy and for the preservation of its loftiest ideals and purposes.

STEPHEN S. WISE

'If These Pillars Fall . . .'

(Daniel Webster's eloquent plea for preservation of America—delivered in 1832):

"Other misfortunes may be borne, or their effects overcome. If disastrous wars should sweep our commerce from the ocean, another generation may renew it; if it exhaust our treasury, future industry may replenish it; if it desolate and lay waste our fields, still, under a new cultivation, they will grow green again, and ripen to future harvests.

"It were but a trifle even if the walls of yonder Capitol were to crumble, if its lofty pillars should fall, and its gorgeous decorations be all covered by the dust of the valley. All of these may be rebuilt.

"But who shall reconstruct the fabric of demolished government?

"Who shall rear again the well-proportioned columns of constitutional liberty?

"Who shall frame together the skillful architecture which unites national sovereignty with State Rights, individual security, and Public prosperity?

"No, if these columns fall, they will be raised not again. Like the Coliseum and the Parthenon, they will be destined to a mournful and melancholy immortality. Bitterer tears, however, will flow over them than ever were shed over the monuments of Roman or Grecian art; for they will be the monuments of a more glorious edifice than Greece or Rome ever saw—the edifice of constitutional American liberty."

They Called It America

God built him a continent of glory, and filled it with treasures untold. He studded it with sweet-flowing fountains, and traced it with long-winding streams. He carpeted it with soft-rolling prairies, and columned it with thundering mountains. He graced it with deep-shadowed forests, and filled them with song.

Then He called unto a thousand peoples, and summoned the bravest among them. They came from the ends of the earth, each bearing a gift and a hope. The glow of adventure was in their eyes, and in their hearts the glory of hope.

And out of the bounty of earth, and the labor of men; out of the longing of heart, and the prayer of souls; out of the memory of ages, and the hopes of the world, God fashioned a nation in love, and blessed it with purpose sublime.

And they called it America.

RABBI ABBA HILLEL SILVER

Those who expect to reap the blessings of freedom must, like men, undergo the fatigues of supporting it.

THOMAS PAINE

We have had the good fortune from the time of the inception of our system of freedom and justice under law to be blessed with sons and daughters who have willingly and courageously risked, or sacrificed their lives . . . in order that this Nation might live and prosper. But the wisdom and sacrifices of yesterday cannot assure the perpetuation of our democratic institutions—they can be preserved only by the constant vigilance of a devoted and dedicated citizenry.

LYNDON B. JOHNSON

A dangerous fallacy is to repudiate freedom in favor of an unknown future. What else but our own sturdy reliance on freedom can explain the unexampled record this country has made? In a period scarcely twice my own lifetime, it (America) has risen from nothingness to become the world's greatest power. It has become the ark of the covenant of freedom.

BERNARD M. BARUCH

A man's feet should be planted in his country, but his eyes should survey the world.

GEORGE SANTAYANA

Our country is still young and its potential is still enormous. We should remember, as we look toward the future, that the more fully we believe in and achieve freedom and equal opportunity—not simply for ourselves but for others—the greater our accomplishments as a nation will be.

HENRY FORD II

All Over, Over There

Ramrod straight, their faces rigidly expressionless, the four men walked single file from their railroad car across duckboards laid on the muddy clearing of Rethondes in the French forest of Compiègne. One, Major General von Winterfeldt, wore the uniform of the Imperial German Army, another, Captain Vanselow, of the Navy. The other two, Mathias Erzberger and Count Oberndorf, were civilians. Behind them came two younger men, their interpreters. In a moment they all entered a transformed railroad dining car with a large table in the center. There they were saluted by a stern-eyed, mustached man wearing the insignia of a Marshal of France—Ferdinand Foch, Allied Supreme Commander.

It was Friday, November 8, 1918. The great war, the worst war, the war to end wars, was almost over. Or was it? All during September from the Dutch frontier to the Meuse, German armies had reeled backward in unprecedented retreat. The British, attacking in the north, cracked the vaunted Siegfried Line. Americans stormed the Argonne. But in both sectors, by mid-October the offensives had stumbled to a halt. Deep in their barbed wire and bunkers, German machine gunners had lost none of the ferocity that had turned Allied offensives of other years into blood baths.

But behind her still intact though battered armies, Germany was falling apart. Ironically, it was the fault of the Fatherland's greatest soldier, General Erich Ludendorff. In a moment of panic during the September offensives, he had recommended that the Imperial Government seek an armistice. The blind faith in Supreme Headquarters had collapsed. A wave of suicides swept the country. By the time Ludendorff regained his nerve, and decided that his armies could still fight, the civilians had bolted. A new chancellor, Prince Max of Baden, had been appointed, with orders to sue for peace.

While the Prince and his diplomats exchanged probing notes with Woodrow Wilson, Germany plunged toward revolution. Wilson's refusal to negotiate with the Kaiser was the last straw. On November 3, the German Navy mutinied, and on November 7 Bavaria revolted. Communists and socialists were threatening to seize Berlin. It became obvious that if the old order were going to salvage anything, an immediate peace was necessary. So the German delegates came to Compiègne.

The Allies, grimly conscious of their own weariness, were wary of an armistice that might give the German armies the time they needed to regroup and re-equip. They were determined that the very acceptance of an armistic would be a surrender. So Foch, after examining the credentials of the delegates, snapped: "What is the purpose of your visit? What do you want of me?"

Plump Mathias Erzberger, representative of the German political moderates, said they had come to receive *"the proposals of the Allied Powers towards the conclusion of an armistice."*

Foch replied: *"I have no proposals to make."*

There was a pained silence. Then Count Oberndorff said humbly: *"How do you wish us to express ourselves? We are not standing on any form of words. We are ready to say that we ask the conditions of an armistice."*

"Do you wish to ask for an armistice?" barked Foch. *"If so, say so, formally."*

Swallowing hard, the Germans said, *"Yes, that is what we are asking."*

"Good. Then we'll read out to you the conditions on which it can be obtained."

Foch ordered General Maxime Weygand, his chief of staff, to read the terms. They were nothing less than the destruction of Germany as a military power. They were to surrender most of their weapons, their airplanes and fighting ships, even their trains, locomotives and trucks, and permit three Allied bridgeheads on the east bank of the Rhine. "Everyone held his head erect; faces were impassive," Weygand later recalled. "The German General was very pale and looked very sad." Captain von Helldorf, one of the German interpreters, burst into tears when he heard about the bridgeheads on the Rhine.

The Germans asked for an immediate armistice to consider the terms. Foch refused. To take the pressure off, even for a day, might cost thousands of lives later, if the Germans chose to continue fighting. Instead the

"Iron Marshal" ordered attacks on November 9 and 10 to make sure the "Boches" had no respite.

For two more days, soldiers died and the world waited while Captain von Helldorf carried the terms back to Supreme Headquarters. He was held up for five hours on the edge of No Man's Land because his own army insisted on shelling the road down which he had to travel. Now came a frantic 36 hours of telegrams from the Germans, trying to get concessions on trains and trucks and numbers of weapons they needed to bring their armies back and restore order at home. On November 9, the Kaiser abdicated and fled to Holland. In Berlin there was street fighting between loyalists and revolutionists.

The Allies made some modest concessions. Finally, at eight p.m. on November 10, a wireless message reached Foch's headquarters. "The German government accepts the conditions of the armistice communicated to it on November 8."

The cease-fire was set for 11 a.m. on November 11. Until that precise moment, both sides kept up the senseless slaughter on the Western Front. In a small village east of Valenciennes, on armistice morning, a British patrol found a wounded German lieutenant propped against a wall. In perfect English he told his captors that the German rearguard had left two hours before. The patrol signaled their battalion forward, and the British formed up and marched into the village square.

Instantly, from all sides, machine guns opened up on them, killing or wounding over 100 men before they could find shelter. The rest of the battalion went through the village, shooting every German they found, including the treacherous lieutenant. "They fought coldly and skillfully when the moment of their own deaths approached," a British historian of the day tells us, "intent only upon taking as many as possible of their attackers with them."

At 10:50 a.m., at Lessines, the British ended the war with a cavalry charge. A staff general decided it was necessary to seize a bridgehead over the river Dendre, and sent a squadron of the 7th Dragoons forward at full gallop to take it. German machine gunners, under orders to keep shooting until 11 a.m., opened up and left men and horses in a bloody tangle.

In the American sector, the Negro 92nd Division, in action for the first time on November 10, had lost over 1,000 men in see-saw fighting around the Bois de Fréhaut. On Armistice morning they attacked again, and captured another . . .

French wood, the Bois de la Voirotte, before 11 a.m. Elsewhere along the American lines the Germans spent the morning dumping their reserve supply of artillery shells on the doughboys, who replied in kind. The Germans ceased firing at 11, but the Americans kept up a sporadic bombardment for almost another hour. Each gun crew wanted to say they had fired the last shot of the war.

Only in the French sectors of the front was it quiet. One French officer recalled: "Walking along the trenches several hours after the armistice, I was surprised to see all our soldiers at their listening posts or in their shelters as if the war was still on."

The German reaction was different. They charged out of their trenches, throwing their hats in the air and in the evening blew up their ammunition dumps and fired away all their star shells. "They were all eager to engage in conversation with our soldiers," the same French officer says, "but to their intense surprise were disdainfully ignored by them." Many German soldiers had no idea they had lost the war. They thought revolutionary governments in France, England and Germany had arranged the truce.

On the British and American fronts, there was more fraternization. "Men formed groups," one writer recalls, "and stared at other groups forming not so far away in space, but until that moment divided from them by hatred and the bar of war. Slowly, almost shyly, the groups approached each other, but often they would halt some few yards apart, while each member scanned the faces of the men opposite, watching for the flash of ferocity they had learned to associate with the alien uniform. Then some movement or expression by one of them would break the tension and the groups would mingle, shaking hands, all talking excitedly in an effort to break the incomprehension, exchanging souvenirs. . . ."

At Allied headquarters, Marshal Foch composed final order of the day:

"Soldiers of the Allied Armies, after having resolutely checked the enemy, you have for months with untiring faith and energy attacked him ceaselessly.

"You have won the greatest battle in history and saved the most sacred cause, the liberty of the world.

"Be proud. You have pinned immortal glory to your flags.

"Posterity will always remember you gratefully."

—Thomas J. Fleming

Reprinted from THIS WEEK MAGAZINE / July 4, 1965

The sheet-anchor of the Ship of State is the common school. Teach, first and last, Americanism. Let no youth leave the school without being thoroughly grounded in the history, the principles, and the incalculable blessings of American liberty. Let the boys be the trained soldiers of constitutional freedom, the girls the intelligent lovers of freemen.

—Chauncey M. Depew

Home on the Range

Imagine the cowboys out on the wide, sky-swept ranges, sitting around a brushwood fire in the evening, singing this song. Americans everywhere know it now. You have probably sung it yourself.

Oh, give me a home where the buffalo roam,
Where the deer and the antelope play,
Where seldom is heard a discouraging word,
And the skies are not cloudy all day.

REFRAIN

Home, home on the range,
Where the deer and the antelope play,
Where seldom is heard a discouraging word,
And the skies are not cloudy all day.

How often at night when the heavens are bright
With the light of the glittering stars,
Have I stood there amazed and asked as I gazed
If their glory exceeds that of ours.

REFRAIN

Oh, give me a land where the bright diamond sand
Flows leisurely down the stream;
Where the graceful white swan goes gliding along
Like a maid in a heavenly dream.

REFRAIN

Then I would not exchange my home on the range,
Where the deer and the antelope play,
Where seldom is heard a discouraging word,
And the skies are not cloudy all day.

REFRAIN

America is God's crucible, the great Melting-Pot where all the races of Europe are melting and reforming! Here you stand, good folk, think I, when I see them at Ellis Island, here you stand in your fifty groups, with your fifty languages and histories, and your fifty blood hatreds and rivalries. But you won't be long like that, brothers, for these are the fires of God you've come to—these are the fires of God. A fig for your feuds and vendettas! Germans and Frenchmen, Irishmen and Englishmen, Jews and Russians—into the Crucible with you all! God is making the American. The real American has not yet arrived. He is only in the crucible, I tell you—he will be the fusion of all races, the common superman.

—ISRAEL ZANGWILL

MESSAGE TO UNITED NATIONS DELEGATES

I propose that God should be openly and audibly invoked at the United Nations in accordance with any one of the religious faiths which are represented here. I do so in the conviction that we cannot make the United Nations into a successful instrument of God's peace without God's help, and that with his help we cannot fail.

HENRY CABOT LODGE, JR.

GOETHALS, THE PROPHET ENGINEER

A man went down to Panama,
Where many a man had died,
To slit the sliding mountains
And lift the eternal tide;
A man stood up in Panama,
And the mountains stood aside.

For a poet wrought in Panama
With a continent for his theme,
And he wrote with flood and fire
To forge a planet's dream,
And the derricks rang his dithyrambs
And his stanzas roared in steam.

Where old Balboa bent his gaze
He leads the liners through,
And the Horn that tossed Magellan
Bellows a far halloo,
For where the navies never sailed
Steamed Goethals and his crew.

So nevermore the tropic routes
Need poleward warp and veer,
But on through the Gates of Goethals
The steady keels shall steer,
Where the tribes of man are led toward
peace
By the prophet engineer.

PERCY MAC KAYE

I AM THE FLAG

I am the flag of the United States of America.

I was born on June 14, 1777, in Philadelphia.

There the Continental Congress adopted my stars and stripes as the national flag.

My thirteen stripes alternating red and white, with a union of thirteen white stars in a field of blue, represented a new constellation, a new nation dedicated to the personal and religious liberty of mankind.

Today fifty stars signal from my union, one for each of the fifty sovereign states in the greatest constitutional republic the world has ever known.

My colors symbolize the patriotic ideals and spiritual qualities of the citizens of my country.

My red stripes proclaim the fearless courage and integrity of American men and boys and the self-sacrifice and devotion of American mothers and daughters.

My white stripes stand for liberty and equality for all.

My blue is the blue of heaven, loyalty, and faith.

I represent these eternal principles: liberty, justice, and humanity.

I embody American freedom: freedom of speech, religion, assembly, the press, and the sanctity of the home.

I typify that indomitable spirit of determination brought to my land by Christopher Columbus and by all my forefathers—the Pilgrims, Puritans, settlers at Jamestown and Plymouth.

I am as old as my nation.

I am a living symbol of my nation's law: the Constitution of the United States and the Bill of Rights.

I voice Abraham Lincoln's philosophy: "A government of the people, by the people, for the people."

I stand guard over my nation's schools, the seedbed of good citizenship and true patriotism.

I am displayed in every schoolroom throughout my nation; every schoolyard has a flag pole for my display.

Daily thousands upon thousands of boys and girls pledge their allegiance to me and my country.

I have my own law—Public Law 829, "The Flag Code"—which definitely states my correct use and display for all occasions and situations.

I have my special day, Flag Day. June 14 is set aside to honor my birth.

Americans, I am the sacred emblem of your country. I symbolize your birthright, your heritage of liberty purchased with blood and sorrow.

I am your title deed of freedom, which is yours to enjoy and hold in trust for posterity.

If you fail to keep this sacred trust inviolate, if I am nullified and destroyed, you and your children will become slaves to dictators and despots.

Eternal vigilance is your price of freedom.

As you see me silhouetted against the peaceful skies of my country, remind yourself that I am the flag of your country, that I stand for what you are—no more, no less.

Guard me well, lest your freedom perish from the earth.

Dedicate your lives to those principles for which I stand: "One nation under God, indivisible, with liberty and justice for all."

I was created in freedom. I made my first appearance in a battle for human liberty.

God grant that I may spend eternity in my "land of the free and the home of the brave" and that I shall ever be known as "Old Glory," the flag of the United States of America.

RUTH APPERSON ROUS

There is nothing wrong with America that the faith, love of freedom, intelligence, and energy of her citizens cannot cure.

DWIGHT D. EISENHOWER

☆ ☆ ☆

D-DAY ORDER

(JUNE 6, 1944)

Soldiers, sailors, and airmen of the Allied expeditionary force: You are about to embark upon a great crusade toward which we have striven these many months. The eyes of the world are upon you. The hopes and prayers of liberty-loving peoples everywhere march with you.

You will bring about the destruction of the German war machine, the elimination of Nazi tyranny over the oppressed peoples of Europe, and security for ourselves in a free world.

Your task will not be an easy one. Your enemy is well trained, well equipped, and battle-hardened. He will fight savagely.

But this is the year 1944. Much has happened since the Nazi triumphs of 1940-41.

The United Nations have inflicted upon the Germans great defeat in open battle man to man. Our air offensive has seriously reduced their strength in the air and their capacity to wage war on the ground.

Our home fronts have given us an overwhelming superiority in weapons and munitions of war and placed at our disposal great reserves of trained fighting men.

The tide has turned.

The free men of the world are marching together to victory. I have full confidence in your courage, devotion to duty, and skill in battle.

We will accept nothing less than full victory.

Good luck, and let us all beseech the blessings of Almighty God upon this great and noble undertaking.

DWIGHT D. EISENHOWER

Never in history have a nation and people had the opportunity that we now have to display greatness.

RALPH J. BUNCHE

If civilization is to survive, we must cultivate the science of human relationships—the ability of all peoples, of all kinds, to live together in the same world at peace.

FRANKLIN D. ROOSEVELT

This generation of Americans has a rendezvous with destiny.

FRANKLIN D. ROOSEVELT

This was the American Dream: a sanctuary on the earth for individual man: a condition in which he could be free not only of the old established closed-corporation hierarchies of arbitrary power which had oppressed him as a mass, but free of that mass into which the hierarchies of church and state had compressed and held him individually thralled and individually impotent.

WILLIAM FAULKNER

This is the Voice of Freedom, General MacArthur speaking. People of the Philippines: I have returned.

—Douglas MacArthur

Götterdämmerung in Germany

On April 30, 1945, while Russian shells smashed Berlin to rubble above his head, Adolf Hitler committed suicide in his bunker. Around him the Third Reich, the empire that was supposed to last a thousand years, was in chaos. In April the Western allies had taken over 1,650,000 prisoners. But as many as 2,000,000 well-armed German soldiers were still in the field, fighting under generals who had taken an oath of obedience to the *Führer*. How would they react to Hitler's successor?

On April 21, Goering had left Berlin for Bavaria and two days later wired Hitler he would assume the role of Führer unless he heard otherwise within hours. This defection was followed by the trusted Himmler's overtures to the Allies through neutral Sweden on April 29, the same day the German forces in Italy surrendered.

Both actions infuriated Hitler, who had decided to commit suicide. He made out a will and political testament. In the latter, he expelled Goering and Himmler from the Nazi Party and stripped them of all their offices. Then he named as his successor Grand Admiral Karl Doenitz.

Doenitz took over the government on May 1 with an emotional announcement on Radio Hamburg: "German Wehrmacht! My Comrades! The *Führer* has fallen . . . One of the greatest heroes in German history has passed away." Doenitz declared he would continue "the struggle against Bolshevism until the fighting troops and the hundreds of thousands of families in Eastern Germany have been preserved from enslavement or destruction." He added that he would "continue to wage war on the British and Americans in so far and for so long as they hinder me in the prosecution of the fight against Bolshevism."

Doenitz thus revealed the last card in the Nazi hand. They hoped to drive a wedge between the Russians and the Western Allies. General Dwight D. Eisenhower, operating from a grimy technical college in Reims (dubbed by correspondents "the little red schoolhouse"), warned all his commanders that any surrender offers beyond the tactical (local) level must be made to him. Meanwhile, the Wehrmacht's generals flatly refused to take an oath of allegiance to Doenitz.

That forced the Admiral to move quickly. On May 3, his representative, Admiral Hans von Friedeburg, arrived at Field Marshal Bernard L. Montgomery's headquarters in north Germany, only a few steps ahead of General Gunter Blumentritt, who was about to surrender German units in the area.

Von Friedeburg promptly offered to surrender three German armies facing the Russians between Berlin and Rostock on the Baltic. Montgomery turned him down, and the British coolly asked the Admiral if he knew what the military situation was. When they showed him on their maps what Germany had left, the Admiral burst into tears. He became so anxious to get back to Doenitz, who was no more in touch with reality, that he blurted out in English: "Hurry up, hurry up—time is money."

The next day, May 4, von Friedeburg returned with the authority to surrender unconditionally all the German forecs in northwest Germany, Holland, and Denmark. With Eisenhower's approval, Montgomery accepted. On May 5, German Army Group G, fighting in the Austrian Alps, surrendered on its own. Admiral von Friedeburg, meanwhile, finally arrived at Eisenhower's headquarters. With the separate surrender in northwest Germany accomplished, Doenitz's plan to play for time seemed to be working.

But Eisenhower gave Admiral von Friedeburg the first of several shocks. He told him flatly that he would accept the surrender of all German forces on the Western Front and Norway only if it included surrender on the Eastern Front at the same time. German troops were to stay where they were, hand over their arms intact and give up on the spot.

Von Friedeburg hedged frantically. The longer he could delay, the more German units could fall back far enough from the Russian front to qualify legitimately as American prisoners. But Eisenhower was determined not to break faith with the Russians, who were already showing signs of distrust.

Grimly, the Americans gave the Admiral another briefing on the military situation, and again he burst into tears. Doenitz then sent General Alfred Jodl, the German Army's chief of staff, to reinforce him on May 6. Jodl's first offer was the now familiar surrender only on the Western Front and that the surrender be signed after 48 hours since time was needed to get the order down to outlying units. Bluntly Eisenhower told Jodl that unless Germany agreed to unconditional surrender on both fronts, immediately, he would seal the American lines, and refuse to admit the streams of individual German soldiers and civilians fleeing westward.

"Eisenhower insists that we sign today," Jodl radioed Doenitz on the evening of May 6. ". . . I see no alternative—chaos or surrender." Doenitz spent half the night in a frantic final effort to come up with another delay. Not until after midnight on May 7 did he give Jodl power to sign with the proviso all fighting stop 48 hours after midnight (midnight, May 8–9). Eisenhower concurred.

The final scene took place in the SHAEF war room. At 2:29 a.m. on the morning of May 7, the representatives of France and Britain arrived, followed by General Ivan Susloparoff, Russia's liaison officer at SHAEF, and finally by the Germans, Jodl and von Friedeburg, and General Walter Bedell Smith, Eisenhower's Chief of Staff. Eisenhower did not appear.

The document was simply a short Act of Military Surrender, which stipulated that appropriate German officers would ratify the agreement at another time and place. Each representative signed four copies. Jodl spoke the last words for Germany: "With this signature the German people and the German armed forces are, for better or worse, delivered into the victors' hands. In this war, which has lasted more than five years, both have achieved and suffered more than perhaps any other people in the world. In this hour I can only express the hope that the victors will treat them with generosity."

A noble speech, if it had not come from the man who had condemned his fellow generals to hideous deaths for attempting to assassinate the *Führer* in 1944, counseled terror bombing of English cities, and signed orders to shoot commandos and prisoners of war.

At 2:41 the papers were signed, and the German envoys were escorted down the hall to meet Eisenhower. Sternly, he asked them if they fully understood the terms. Yes. Would Germany carry them out? Yes. The Germans departed. Air Marshal Arthur Tedder of Great Britain, Deputy Supreme Commander, brought Eisenhower the two pens used in the signing. Ike held up the pens to form a victorious V. He then sent a simple, typically undramatic message to the Combined Chiefs of Staff: "The Mission of this Allied Force was fulfilled at 0241 local time, May 7, 1945."

At 3:05, as Bedell Smith got into his car, he said: "Fini la guerre." He was not quite correct. The Russians, after first giving Susloparoff permission to sign, revoked it and announced they would not consider any surrender real until Marshal Zhukov signed, too—preferably in Berlin. Stalin, meanwhile, was urging Roosevelt and Churchill not to make any announcement until the Berlin signing. But the Allied leaders decided it was impossible to keep the surrender a secret.

Eisenhower decided not to go to Berlin, lest he become embroiled with the Russians in arguments over precedence in the final signing. Instead, he sent Air Marshal Tedder, and let Zhukov preside over what was for the rest of the world an anti-climax.

Numerous German units, however, kept on fighting the Russians and trying to retreat west. Ike ended this by ordering all approaches to his lines blocked.

In a private message to General George C. Marshall, Ike summed up the wishful hopes and honorable intentions which motivated the Americans: "This meeting (at Berlin) completely concurred in by the Russians, finally relieves my mind of the anxiety that I have had due to the danger of misunderstandings at the very last minute . . . To be perfectly frank, the four days just past have taken more out of me and my staff than the past eleven months of this campaign."

—Thomas J. Fleming

THIS WEEK MAGAZINE / July 4, 1965

If any one desires to know the leading and paramount object of my public life, the preservation of this Union will furnish him the key.

—*Henry Clay*

FAITHFUL AT DUTY

Nearly one hundred years ago, there was a day of remarkable gloom and darkness, still known as the Dark Day—a day when the light of the sun was slowly extinguished as if by an eclipse.

The Legislature of Connecticut was in session, and as the members saw the unexpected and unaccountable darkness coming on, they shared in the general awe and terror. It was supposed by many that the last day, the day of judgment, had come. Someone, in the consternation of the hour, moved an adjournment.

Then there arose an old Puritan legislator, Davenport Stanford, who said that if the last day had come he desired to be found at his post of duty, and therefore moved that candles be brought so that the House could proceed with its business.

So, my son, when in the conflict of life the cloud and the darkness come, stand unflinchingly by your post; remain faithful to the discharge of your duty.

ROBERT E. LEE

V-J DAY, 1945: *The elaborate ceremony aboard the* Missouri *was designed to underline defeat of Japan's warlords. At left: MacArthur*

The Rising Sun Goes Down

Emperor Hirohito had made his decision. But a gang of fanatics made a desperate attempt to cancel surrender and launch fresh slaughter

In Japan, the surrender drama took place in a nation whose army was essentially intact, and whose government was firmly in control. Not the fearful chaos of the B-29 firebomb raids, the cataclysmic blows of two atomic bombs, or the entry of the Russians into the war had convinced the militarists dominating the Japanese cabinet that surrender was the only choice.

The Japanese morning papers on August 11, two days after the second atomic bomb hit Nagasaki, carried instructions to the officers and men of the army from the Minister of War, General Korechika Anami:

"The only thing for us to do is to fight doggedly to the end in this holy war for the defense of our divine land . . . though it may mean chewing grass, eating dirt and sleeping in the field, a resolute fight will surely reveal a way out of a desperate situation."

Anami meant every word of it. For weeks a peace party in Japan's Supreme Council for the Direction of the War had, with the cautious support of Emperor Hirohito, tried to work out acceptable terms for ending the war. The Army and Navy chiefs adamantly refused to cooperate. The Americans probably had only had two atom bombs and would not dare use such a weapon when they invaded. Honor demanded a final battle on Japanese soil. Japanese history proved conclusively that the way to victory was to "lure" the enemy ashore and annihilate them as the original Kamikaze "divine wind" had destroyed the hordes of Kublai Khan in 1281 A.D.

Backing up this argument were 5,350 Kamikaze planes and another 12,000 usable aircraft, plus 5,000 men in training in the Kamikaze Corps. Perhaps more important, the militarists were prepared to assassinate

Reprinted from THIS WEEK MAGAZINE / July 4, 1965

anyone who disagreed. Years later, MacArthur asked Hirohito why he had not taken a more active role in pushing Japan toward peace. He replied by drawing his finger across his throat.

It took considerable Imperial courage to intervene, but Hirohito summoned the Supreme Council to a meeting in the royal air-raid shelter at 11 a.m. on August 14. He pointed out that the Americans had assured Japan that the Emperor could remain on his throne, thus removing one of the militarists' chief objections to surrender. He, therefore, asked his ministers to "bear the unbearable" in order to "preserve the state as a state." He admitted that the decision would be a shock to the armed forces and said he was ready to appeal directly to the troops, and to broadcast his decision to the people—both unprecedented in Japanese tradition.

That afternoon, the Emperor made a recording of his "Imperial rescript" for broadcast the following day. That evening his ministers asked the Swiss government to relay to the Allied governments acceptance of their surrender terms, which had been communicated earlier.

The news reached Washington late on the afternoon of August 14. President Truman joyously announced it to the nation at 7 o'clock that night, and the country went on a two-day spree. While Americans danced in the streets, fanatics in Tokyo came within inches of undoing the peace before it began. During the night of 14-15 August, they went to Lieutenant General Takeshi Mori, commanding the elite Imperial Guards Division, and told him to order his men to disobey the surrender order. Mori refused and was assassinated.

The plotters now prepared forged orders, directing the division to seal off the Imperial palace and seize the recording of the Emperor's surrender message. Other assassins attacked the homes of Prime Minister Suzuki and Marquis Kido, a leader of the peace party. At dawn one of the Kamikaze squadrons from Atsugi Airfield flew over Tokyo, dropping leaflets proclaiming that this was "Gyokusai"— the final day of reckoning.

Fortunately, the Emperor had already taken the precaution of summoning the senior military commanders in Japan, and asking them to make sure the armed forces obeyed his decision. General Tanaka, commander of the Eastern Army District Area, thus hurried to the palace and took personal charge of the rebellious Imperial Guards. By 8 a.m. the coup was foiled. Tanaka committed hara-kiri. So did Minister of War Anami, four of the principal conspirators, and Vice Admiral Takijino Onishi, father of the Kamikaze Corps.

At noon, Hirohito's musical, high-pitched voice informed his people that the war was over, though the word "surrender" was carefully omitted.

For the next two weeks, General Douglas MacArthur, designated Supreme Allied Commander by Truman, worked with the Japanese on arrangements for the formal surrender. At first there was talk of a prior naval occupation, but MacArthur objected violently, and it was arranged for the 11th Airborne Division to land at Atsugi Airfield, 25 miles from Tokyo, at around the same time the fleet sent marines ashore in Tokyo Bay. Meanwhile, there was trouble with Russia, which fought on for several days in Manchuria, driving down into China to seize vital road junctions. Moscow also demanded the right to occupy Hokkaido, the northernmost of the main Japanese islands, and thus carve up Japan as the conquerors had carved up Germany. It was rebuffed by Truman.

Inside Japan, there were still ominous rumblings. Only a visit from a member of the Imperial family dissuaded the Kamikaze squadrons at Atsugi from assaulting the American fleet as it began to steam into Tokyo Bay on August 28. Their ire may have been aroused by a daredevil pilot from the carrier *Yorktown,* who landed alone at the field on August 27 and had the Japanese ground crews paint a large sign: "Welcome to the U.S. Army from the Third Fleet."

Both MacArthur and Truman wanted the surrender ceremony to be impressive, to make it clear to the Japanese people that their warlords had been defeated. They decided against holding it in Tokyo, for fear of arousing the fanatics. Stalin recommended holding it as far away from Japan as possible, preferably in Manila. The Americans finally chose the deck of the battleship *Missouri,* flagship of Admiral William F. ("Bull") Halsey's Third Fleet, surrounded in Toyko Bay by 257 other battlewagons, carriers, cruisers, destroyers and smaller craft.

The morning of the formal signing on September 2 was gloomy and overcast. The first dignitaries arrived aboard the *Missouri* around 7 a.m. General MacArthur and Admiral Nimitz came aboard, and at 8:56 the Japanese delegation arrived. They were led by the Foreign Minister, Mamoru Shigemitsu, and General Yoshijiro Umezu, chief of the Army General Staff. There were also three representatives each from the Foreign Office, the Army and the Navy.

General Umezu had threatened to commit hara-kiri when he was ordered to participate, and only agreed on the personal intercession of the Emperor.

Shigemitsu had a wooden leg and had trouble getting up the *Missouri*'s steep ladder. The delegation stood immobile, facing the surrender table, while the ship's chaplain spoke an invocation over the public-address system and a record played "The Star-Spangled Banner."

Precisely at nine, General MacArthur appeared with Admirals Nimitz and Halsey. With them were two emaciated men—Lt. Gen. Jonathan M. Wainwright, captured at Corregidor in 1942, and Lt. Gen. Sir

Arthur E. Percival, captured at the fall of Singapore in 1942. MacArthur had ordered them flown from prison camps in Manchuria. MacArthur spoke briefly, expressing the *"earnest hope . . . that from this solemn occasion a better world will emerge."* Deeply moved by his words, one Japanese delegate, Toshikazu Kase, later said he felt MacArthur turned the quarterdeck into "an altar of peace."

The General now pointed to a chair at the table on which the surrender documents rested, bound in green for the victors, black (a ceremonial color in Japan) for the vanquished. *"I now invite the representative of the Emperor of Japan and the Japanese Government and the Japanese Imperial General Headquarters to sign the instrument of surrender at the places designated,"* MacArthur said.

Leaning heavily on his cane, Shigemitsu hobbled forward and sat down. He had trouble getting his wooden leg under the table. Completely rattled, he pulled a watch from his pocket instead of a pen, fumbled with papers in his coat, pulled out a second watch, and finally a pen. "Sutherland," MacArthur said to his chief of staff, "show him where to sign." General Sutherland did so. General Umezu signed next, without incident.

Then MacArthur sat down and signed, using no less than five pens; one he gave to Wainwright, another to Percival, a third was for the U.S. archives, a fourth for West Point. The fifth belonged to Mrs. MacArthur.

Admiral Nimitz now signed, followed by the allied delegates. MacArthur ended the ceremony at 9:25 with two terse sentences: "Let us pray that peace be now restored to the world and that God will preserve it always. These proceedings are now closed." As the Japanese departed the sun broke through, and a flight of 450 carrier planes, followed by several hundred Army aircraft, swept over the *Missouri.*

That evening, on the deck of the battleship, *Duke of York,* massed bands of all British ships played a sunset hymn, as the flags of all the Allied nations were slowly lowered from the signal yards. The hymn was John Ellerton's "The Day Thou Gavest, Lord, is Ended." Its words were an appropriate finale to the greatest war in history:

"The Day thou gavest, Lord, is ended,
The darkness falls at thy behest;
To thee our morning hymns ascended,
Thy praise shall sanctify our rest.

So be it, Lord; thy throne shall never,
Like earth's proud empires, pass away;
Thy kingdom stands, and grows for ever,
Till all thy creatures own thy sway."

—THOMAS J. FLEMING

As long as our Government is administered for the good of the people, and is regulated by their will; as long as it secures to us the rights of persons and of property, liberty of conscience and of the press, it will be worth defending. ANDREW JACKSON

Horizon 1976

UNITED NATIONS CHARTER PREAMBLE

We, the peoples of the United Nations, determined to save succeeding generations from the scourge of war, which twice in our lifetime has brought untold sorrow to mankind, and

To reaffirm faith in fundamental human rights, in the dignity and worth of the human person, in the equal rights of men and women and of nations large and small, and

To establish conditions under which justice and respect for the obligations arising from treaties and other sources of international law can be maintained, and

To promote social progress and better standards of life in larger freedom, and for these ends

To practice tolerance and live together in peace with one another as good neighbors, and

To unite our strength to maintain international peace and security, and

To insure, by the acceptance of principles and the institution of methods, that armed force shall not be used, save in the common interest, and

To employ international machinery for the promotion of the economic and social advancement of all peoples, have resolved to combine our efforts to accomplish these aims.

ADOPTED IN SAN FRANCISCO

JUNE 26, 1945

THE FOUR FREEDOMS

In the future days, which we seek to make secure, we look forward to a world founded upon four essential human freedoms.

The first is freedom of speech and expression—everywhere in the world.

The second is freedom of every person to worship God in his own way—everywhere in the world.

The third is freedom from want—which, translated into world terms, means economic understandings which will secure to every nation a healthy peacetime life for its inhabitants—everywhere in the world.

The fourth is freedom from fear—which, translated into world terms, means a world-wide reduction of armaments to such a point and in such a thorough fashion that no nation will be in a position to commit an act of physical aggression against any neighbor—anywhere in the world.

That is no vision of a distant millennium. It is a definite basis for a kind of world attainable in our own time and generation. That kind of world is the very antithesis of the so-called new order of tyranny which the dictators seek to create with the crash of a bomb.

—Franklin D. Roosevelt

The Declaration of Independence gave liberty not alone to the people of this country, but hope to all the world, for all future time. It was that which gave promise that in due time the weights would be lifted from the shoulders of all men, and that all should have an equal chance. This is the sentiment embodied in the Declaration of Independence.

ABRAHAM LINCOLN

The American Animal . . . is nothing but the big Honest Majority, that you might find in any country. He is no politician, he is not a 100% American, he is not any organization, either uplift or downfall . . . In fact, all I can find out about him is that he is just normal . . . This normal breed is so far in the majority that there is no use to worry about the others. They are a lot of mavericks and strays.

—Will Rogers

The Government of the Union is emphatically and truly a government of the people. In form and in substance it emanates from them. Its powers are granted by them and are to be exercised directly on them and for their benefit.

JOHN MARSHALL

For All Mankind

(Apollo 11)

I'm at the foot of the ladder. The LM foot pads are only depressed in the surface about 1 or 2 inches. Although the surface appears to be very, very fine grained, as you get close to it. It's almost like a powder. Now and then, it's very fine. I'm going to step off the LM now.

That's one small step for a man. One giant leap for mankind.

NEIL A. ARMSTRONG
10:56 p.m. (E.D.T.), July 20, 1969

THE EAGLE HAS LANDED

ALDRIN—Beautiful, beautiful.

ARMSTRONG—Isn't that something. Magnificent sight down here.

ALDRIN—Magnificent desolation.

CAPCOM—Yes, indeed. They've got the flag up and you can see the stars and stripes on the lunar surface.

COLUMBIA—Beautiful. Just beautiful.

Neil and Buzz, I am talking to you by telephone from the Oval Room at the White House. And this certainly has to be the most historic telephone call ever made. I just can't tell you how proud we all are of what you . . . for every American, this has to be the proudest day of our lives. And for people all over the world, I am sure they, too, join with Americans, in recognizing what a feat this is. Because of what you have done, the heavens have become a part of man's world. And as you talk to us from the Sea of Tranquility, it inspires us to double our efforts to bring peace and tranquility to earth. For one priceless moment, in the whole history of man, all the people on this earth are truly one. One in their pride in what you have done. And one in our prayers, that you will return safely to earth.

PRESIDENT NIXON

Thank you, Mr. President. It's a great honor and privilege for us to be here representing not only the United States but men of peace of all nations. And with interest and a curiosity and a vision for the future. It's an honor for us to be able to participate here today.

ARMSTRONG

As I stand out here on the wonders of the unknown at Hadley, I sort of realize there is a fundamental truth to our nature. Man must explore. And this is exploration at its greatest.

Apollo 15 Astronaut Dave Scott
TIME, AUGUST 9, 1971

APOLLO 16

Astronauts John Young, Charles Duke and Ken Mattingly arrived for their red-carpet welcome on the *Ticonderoga's* flight deck, "By golly," said Young, "you taxpayers—we taxpayers—got your money's worth."

No doubt about it. For all the problems they had encountered on the way to the moon and in the process of settling up their experiments, the Apollo 16 astronauts scored a scientific triumph. Young and Duke spent 20 hours and 14 minutes prowling the lunar surface, only three-quarters of an hour short of their original goal. They also collected so much moon material that they nearly ran out of collection bags. Most significant of all, the next to last Apollo mission has already given scientists valuable new details about the terrain that makes up more than 80% of the lunar surface: the rugged and ancient highlands.

On the eve of their splashdown, the astronauts answered reporters' questions relayed by Mission Control during a televised press conference. "We've seen as much in ten days," Young concluded, "as most people see in ten lifetimes." He may have been too modest. For all of the mission's mishaps, the information gathered during the flight of Apollo 16 may well enable man to "see" back to the very beginnings of his world.

"The frontiers of the unknown are man's eternal frontiers," astronaut John W. Young Jr., 41, told the crowd after he stepped out on a red carpet, to U.S. soil for the first time since Apollo 16 left Cape Kennedy April 16.

(April 27, 1972)

"Those who came before us made certain that this country rode the first waves of the industrial revolution, the first waves of modern invention and the first wave of nuclear power. And this generation does not intend to founder in the backwash of the coming age of space. We mean to be part of it—we mean to lead it."

PRESIDENT JOHN F. KENNEDY

Apollo & Beyond

Three billion years ago, the Moon summoned life out of its first home, the sea, and led it onto the empty land. For as it drew the tides across the barren continents of primeval Earth, their daily rhythm exposed to sun and air the creatures of the shallows. Most perished—but some adapted to the new and hostile environment. The conquest of the land had begun. We shall never know when this happened, on the shores of what vanished sea. There were no eyes or cameras to record so obscure, so inconspicuous an event. Now, the Moon calls again—and this time life responds with a roar that shakes earth and sky. When a Saturn V soars spaceward on four thousand tons of thrust, it signifies more than a triumph of technology. It opens the next chapter of Evolution. No wonder that the drama of a launch engages our emotions so deeply. The rising rocket appeals to instincts older than reason; the gulf it bridges is not only that between world and world—but the deeper chasm between heart and brain. If the Moon did not exist, the Apollo Program would still be necessary—to establish the manned "space stations" of the 1970's. Communications and meteorological satellites have proved that many earthly problems can be solved *only* in space. And from thousands of miles above the turning globe, orbiting electronic eyes have already disclosed new resources of land and sea beyond the reach of ground observation. But we cannot exploit the full potential of space until men can operate there. Fifty million dollar satellites have failed because of a single small component—expensive proof that we need repair and maintenance crews in orbit. To get them there cheaply will require spacecraft that—unlike today's rockets—can be flown over and over again. Such reuseable vehicles (perhaps stubby, winged ships that can land at ordinary airfields) are already on the drawing boards. They will be the DC-3's of the Early Space Age—for they will herald the true dawn of interplanetary commerce. The dreams and labors of more than a million men place the first astronauts on the Moon. Behind the armies of engineers and scientists who toiled at Cape Kennedy, Baikonur and Peenemünde stand also the giants of the past—Newton, Galileo, Kepler, Archimedes. . . . Their names—and those of later men like Goddard, Tsiolkovsky, Amundsen, Scott, Byrd—are now engraved on the maps of the Moon. They have been given to the mountains and craters that will be the landmarks of future explorers. Once we have gained a foothold on our single natural satellite—a world as large as Africa, with unknown but certainly immense resources—we will establish permanent bases there. At first, they will be solely for scientific purposes, like those in the Antarctic today, but in time, they may grow to cities, to colonies. (Who could have imagined, five centuries ago, the millions who would one day inhabit the American wilderness?) Yet our Moon's greatest value may be as a stepping-stone to more distant worlds. Here, close to Mother Earth, we will perfect the skills needed for the conquest of Mars and Mercury, and the many moons that orbit giant Jupiter, ringed Saturn. The men behind Apollo are already dreaming of such remoter goals. And the work they do today will be honored in the centuries to come, when their names are written on maps, as yet undrawn, of undiscovered worlds.

Arthur C. Clarke

TREASON FROM WITHIN

A nation can survive its fools, and even the ambitious. But it cannot survive treason from within. An enemy at the gates is less formidable, for he is known and he carries his banners openly. But the traitor moves among those within the gate freely, his sly whispers rustling through all the alleys, heard in the very halls of government itself. For the traitor appears no traitor; he speaks in the accents familiar to his victims, and he wears their face and their garments, and he appeals to the baseness that lies deep in the hearts of all men. He rots the soul of a nation; he works secretly and unknown in the night to undermine the pillars of a city; he infects the body politic so that it can no longer resist. A murderer is less to be feared.

Cicero

☆ ☆ ☆ ☆ ☆

THEY WENT TO CHURCH

One item in which the astronauts were interested was news from their homes. They pressed mission control to call their families and keep tab on their activities.

"APPRECIATE that every day if you could," they said.

In and around the astronaut colony in Houston, the wives and children of the Apollo 12 crew went to church.

Sunday, November 16, 1969

The children of the Ghetto possess all the qualities which make for noble manhood and womanhood; but the Ghetto itself, like an infuriated tigress turning on its young, turns upon and destroys all these qualities, blots out the light and laughter, and moulds those it does not kill into sodden and forlorn creatures, uncouth, degraded, and wretched below the beasts of the field.

—Jack London

AMNESTY FOR DESERTERS?

The only principles of public conduct that are worthy of a gentleman or a man are to sacrifice estate, ease, health, and applause, and even life, to the sacred calls of his country.

These manly sentiments, in private life, make the good citizen; in public life, the patriot and the hero.

February 24, 1761, JAMES OTIS

The Ship of Democracy, which has weathered all storms, may sing through the mutiny of those on board.

Grover Cleveland

MEMORIAL DAY

From out our crowded calendar
One day we pluck to give;
It is the day the Dying pause
To honor those who live.

McLandburgh Wilson

I HEAR AMERICA SINGING

I hear America singing, the varied carols I hear;
Those of mechanics—each one singing his, as it should be, blithe and strong;
The carpenter singing his, as he measures his plank or beam,
The mason singing his, as he makes ready for work, or leaves off work;
The boatman singing what belongs to him in his boat —the deckhand singing on the steamboat deck;
The shoemaker singing as he sits on his bench—the hatter singing as he stands;
The wood-cutter's song—the ploughboy's, on his way in the morning, or at the noon intermission, or at sundown;
The delicious singing of the mother—or of the young wife at work—or of the girl sewing or washing;
Each singing what belongs to him or her, and to none else;
The day what belongs to the day—at night, the party of young fellows, robust, friendly,
Singing, with open mouths, their strong melodious songs.

Walt Whitman

Our history books tell us that the American Revolution ended in Yorktown. But the American Revolution will not be complete until the ideals of independence, equality and freedom which kept men fighting at Valley Forge are a reality not only for Americans but for peoples throughout the world.

Richard M. Nixon
July 4, 1965

And so my fellow Americans: Ask not what your country can do for you—ask what you can do for your country.

—John Fitzgerald Kennedy

IN FLANDERS FIELDS

In Flanders fields the poppies blow
Between the crosses, row on row,
That mark our place; and in the sky
The larks, still bravely singing, fly
Scarce heard amid the guns below.

We are the Dead. Short days ago
We lived, felt dawn, saw sunset glow,
Loved and were loved, and now we lie
In Flanders fields.

Take up our quarrel with the foe:
To you from failing hands we throw
The torch; be yours to hold it high.
If ye break faith with us who die
We shall not sleep, though poppies grow
In Flanders fields.

John McCrae

AMERICA FOR ME

'Tis fine to see the Old World, and travel up and down
Among the famous palaces and cities of renown,
To admire the crumbly castles and the statues of the kings,—
But now I think I've had enough of antiquated things.

So it's home again, and home again, America for me!
My heart is turning home again, and there I long to be
In the land of youth and freedom beyond the ocean bars,
Where the air is full of sunlight and the flag is full of stars.

Oh, London is a man's town, there's power in the air;
And Paris is a woman's town, with flowers in her hair;
And it's sweet to dream in Venice, and it's great to study Rome,
But when it comes to living, there is no place like home.

I like the German fir-woods, in green battalions drilled;
I like the gardens of Versailles with flashing fountains filled;
But, oh, to take your hand, my dear, and ramble for a day
In the friendly western woodland where Nature has her way!

I know that Europe's wonderful, yet something seems to lack!
The Past is too much with her, and the people looking back.
But the glory of the Present is to make the Future free,—
We love our land for what she is and what she is to be.

Oh, it's home again, and home again, America for me!
I want a ship that's westward bound to plough the rolling sea,
To the blessed Land of Room Enough beyond the ocean bars,
Where the air is full of sunlight and the flag is full of stars.

HENRY VAN DYKE

The things that will destroy America are prosperity at any price, peace at any price, safety first instead of duty first, the love of soft living and the get-rich-quick feeling of living.

ARTHUR W. RADFORD

PRIVILEGE AND OBLIGATION

To millions of people all over the world America is a magic name. Here are schools, roads, parks, libraries, and playgrounds; peaceful living and the right to choose our jobs and plan our lives. Such an ample way of life we may too readily assume to be our natural right. But every benefit, every right, was bought for us—at a price. When we think of the cost paid by our forefathers, we begin to realize that living in a great land is a responsibility as well as a privilege. As we share the experiences of Americans past and present, we may discover new reasons for wanting to keep our country the home of the brave and the free and the good.

I'm glad to be dying for England. Other women are sacrificing more—husbands, brothers, sons. I have only my own life to give.

—EDITH CAVELL

A nation never falls but by suicide.

RALPH WALDO EMERSON

One recalls the famous words of the French Henry IV to the cowardly Crillon after the battle of Arques: "Hang yourself, brave Crillon; we fought at Arques and you were not there!"

Says Toynbee, the great historian: "Fourteen out of the twenty-one great civilizations which this earth has known, are now only of interest to the antiquary." God's workshop floor is littered with the broken pieces of those instruments which he could no longer use. One wonders whether Europe and America will be usable instruments, or be thrown away as unusable like Egypt and Babylon and the rest.

"If black America has not written off all of white America, in spite of slavery, lynching, daily humiliation, it seems to me that white people ought to be able to hang in there. Black America has said in a thousand ways that it believes in America. It has said it in slavery; it has said it in war; it has said it in peace. It seems to me now that the time has come for America to say, 'Black Americans, we believe in you.'"

WHITNEY YOUNG

AMERICA'S FUTURE

I look forward to a great future for America—a future in which our country will match its military strength with our moral strength, its wealth with our wisdom, its power with our purpose.

I look forward to an America which will not be afraid of grace and beauty, which will protect the beauty of our natural environment, which will preserve the great old American houses and squares and parks of our national past, and which will build handsome and balanced cities for our future.

I look forward to an America which will reward achievement in the arts as we reward achievement in business or statecraft.

I look forward to an America which will steadily raise the standards of artistic accomplishment and which will steadily enlarge cultural opportunities for all of our citizens.

I look forward to an America which commands respect throughout the world not only for its strength but for its civilization as well. And I look forward to a world which will be safe for democracy and diversity but also for personal distinction.

JOHN F. KENNEDY

I think the true discovery of America is before us. I think the true fulfillment of our spirit, of our people, of our mighty and immortal land, is yet to come. I think the true discovery of our own democracy is still before us. And I think that all these things are certain as the morning, as inevitable as noon. I think I speak for most men living when I say that our America is Here, is Now, and beckons on before us, and that this glorious assurance is not only our living hope, but our dream to be accomplished.

THOMAS WOLFE

Intellectually I know that America is no better than any other country; emotionally I know she is better than every other country.

—SINCLAIR LEWIS

Many times a day I realize how much my own outer and inner life is built upon the labors of my fellowmen, both living and dead, and how earnestly I must exert myself in order to give in return as much as I have received.

—ALBERT EINSTEIN

I LOVE AMERICA

I love America, where truth can be shouted from the housetops, instead of whispered in dismal cellars hidden from the spies and dictators.

I love America, where families can sleep peacefully without fear of secret seizure and torture in some foul prison, or purged in blood for political reasons.

I love America, where men are truly free men; not living in fear of slavery, exile, or involuntary servitude, while their homes are confiscated and loved ones are turned weeping and sorrowing from their doors.

I love America, where there are equal rights for all, and where people are not forced to hate, persecute, or kill because of religion, race, or creed.

I love America, where little children are not forced to suffer for want of bread withheld at the whim of some despot carrying out a plan for greater glory.

I love America, where men can think as they please, and where thought is not regulated by decrees, enforced with bullets and bayonets.

I love America, where there is love, laughter, hope, and opportunity, and not hate, sorrow, dejection, and futility.

I love America despite her present troubles because free men can cure them.

I love America, and I will gladly give my life to preserve the freedom our forefathers created, so that our children and their descendants can forever enjoy blessings we have inherited.

FRANKLIN E. JORDAN

TRIBUTE TO THE FLAG

I have seen the glories of art and architecture and of river and mountain. I have seen the sun set on the Jungfrau and the moon rise over Mont Blanc. But the fairest vision on which these eyes ever rested was the flag of my country in a foreign port. Beautiful as a flower to those who love it, terrible as a meteor to those who hate it, it is the symbol of the power and the glory and the honor of millions of Americans.

—George F. Hoar

PRAYER FROM APOLLO 8

Give us, O God, the vision which can see thy love in the world in spite of human failure. Give us the faith to trust thy goodness in spite of our ignorance and weakness. Give us the knowledge that we may continue to pray with understanding hearts, and show us what each one of us can do to set forward the coming of the day of universal peace.

FRANK BORMAN

A NEW WIND A-BLOWIN'

There's a brand new wind a-blowin' down
that Lincoln road.
There's a brand new hope a-growin' down
where freedom's seeds are sowed.
There's a new truth we'll be knowin' that
will lift our heavy load,
When we find out what free men can really
do.

There's a brand new day a–comin' for the
land called U.S.A.
New tunes we'll be a–strummin' in our
hearts by night and day.
As we march on we'll be hummin', how our
troubles' gone away,
'Cause we've found out what free men can
really do.

And if you feel like dancin' then, why
come on folks, and dance!
And if you feel like prancin' then, why
come on folks, and prance!
'Cause I really ain't romancin' when I say
we've got our chance
To show 'em what free men can really do.

There's a brand new wind a-blowin' thru
a land that's proud and free.
Ev'rywhere there's folks a-wakin' to a
truth that's bound to be.
So let's all pull together for that day
of victory,
And we'll show 'em what free men can
really do!

LANGSTON HUGHES

Men grow when inspired by a high purpose when contemplating vast horizons. The sacrifice of oneself is not very difficult for one burning with the passion for a great adventure.

—Alexis Carrel

The highest flights of charity, devotion, trust, patience, bravery, to which the wings of human nature have spread themselves, have been flown for religious ideals.

WILLIAM JAMES

OTHER WORLDS

Moon Colonies: An observatory on the moon would be a wonderful way to investigate the heavens, because the difficulties of the [Earth's] atmosphere would disappear. The atmosphere is the reason stars twinkle. This effect would be avoided, and one would be much better able to explore the heavens from the moon. Sometime, there might be such an observatory on the moon. I would not exclude the possibility at all.

Mars: I think that, simply because the moon doesn't have any life on it doesn't mean that there may not be life on Mars. If there's life on Mars, it is very probably a different life than on the Earth.

—Harold Urey

Our Heritage

May I remind you that the Constitution of the United States remains the greatest liberal instrument of government that the hand of man has ever written. Keep your government as your servant. Keep the miracle of America the most priceless heritage of future generations. All through our national history, ours has been the mission of freedom, of liberty, of tolerance, of peace and of the stern refusal to accept for ourselves the jealousies, bigotries, and the passions of the old world.

SENATOR KARL MUNDT

Liberty is the only thing you cannot have unless you are willing to give it to others.

WILLIAM ALLEN WHITE

Every American is a free member of a mighty partnership that has at its command all the pooled strength of Western Civilization—spiritual ideals, political experience, social purpose, scientific wealth, industrial prowess.

There is no limit, other than our own resolve, to the temporal goals we set before ourselves—as free individuals joined in a team with our fellows, as a free nation in the community of nations.

DWIGHT D. EISENHOWER

Many generations ago, Benjamin Franklin pointed across the hall of the Constitutional Convention at Philadelphia to the golden half-sun engraved on the back of Washington's chair, and he remarked: "Now, at length, I have the happiness to know that it is a rising, not a setting, sun." And so today, when a single fireball can light the fires of ten thousand suns, we need to reaffirm our faith in America.

NELSON A. ROCKEFELLER

Democracy is not just a word to be shouted at political rallies and then put back into the dictionary after election day. . . . It is a living thing—a human thing—compounded of brains and muscles and heart and soul.

FRANKLIN D. ROOSEVELT

We still have it in our power to rise above the fears, imagined and real, and to shoulder the great burdens which destiny has placed upon us. . . .

HELEN KELLER

While the people of other countries are struggling to establish free institutions, under which man may govern himself, we are in the actual enjoyment of them—a rich inheritance from our fathers.

JAMES K. POLK

In the long view of history, these years are the early summer of America. Our land is young. Our strength is great. Our course is far from run.

LYNDON B. JOHNSON

I like the dreams of the future better than the history of the past.

THOMAS JEFFERSON

In the future days, which we seek to make secure, we look forward to a world founded upon four essential human freedoms. The first is freedom of speech and expression—everywhere in the world. The second is freedom of every person to worship God in his own way—everywhere in the world. The third is freedom from want—everywhere in the world. The fourth is freedom from fear—anywhere in the world!

—Franklin Delano Roosevelt

Index